"An incredible book—I feel so much wiser after having read it. Laura Jiménez respects the intelligence of her reader too much to sugarcoat the truth and we are all better readers, writers and humans because of it. I wish everyone in the children's literature community could read and learn from this smart, perceptive and insightful book; not only does Laura open our eyes but she also gives us tools to keep us alert. For those of us who believe that children's literature can change the world for the better, this is an essential guidebook."

—Grace Lin
Children's Literature Legacy author and illustrator

"Reading *Judging a Book By More Than Its Cover* feels like a coffee date with your favorite professor. Dr. Jiménez gently walks readers through our own biases while imparting the knowledge to help us grapple with the reasons to challenge our assumptions and engage with children's literature that meet both the moment and readers who aren't often considered when book choices are made."

—Jill M. Hermann-Wilmarth, PhD
professor in the College of Education and Human Development at Western Michigan University

"Warm, funny, and endlessly readable, this book makes selecting and teaching with diverse children's literature feel essential and doable. With sharp insights, real life examples, and plenty of humor, Laura invites educators into conversations that can help change our schools and our world."

—Caitlin L. Ryan

"*Judging a Book By More Than Its Cover* is the definitive guide to becoming the advocate your students need. The book introduces the vital concept of looking at our shelves with fresh, critical eyes, making visible the need to move past our own nostalgia to ensure the stories we share with students honor and reflect the diversity of their lives. It provides the political clarity we need to protect our students' right to read, pushing past fear to focused advocacy.

This blurb could state, read this book because it is brilliant, informative, and helpful in understanding the back story to the back story, and why that matters in your teaching. But the real reason you should read this book is because it is authentic and written with the care of an expert who respects the reader as an agentive, intelligent, compassionate educator who has the gumption to want to engage readers with books that will transform their lives. *Judging a Book By More Than Its Cover* has set a new bar for how I want to engage with books as a thinker. As strange as it is to write, reading this book reminded me of late nights at my computer with a glass of red wine and Cheetos—elevated content layered with the stuff you reach for because it just works."

—Detra M. Price
The Ohio State University

"Imagine a deeply wise, real-talking best friend gives you decades of scholarship about children's literature in a fun-to-read (often funny!), pithy, accessible guide with tons of examples and resources to make what you learn actionable. Expect you will be challenged often. But then, you will be well-informed to make decisions about what texts to include and exclude in your curriculum, and your students will be better served because of it. Whether you're a professor planning your children's lit undergrad or graduate course, a school librarian, a classroom teacher, a literacy coach, a school or district leader, or a consultant, you need this book."

—Jennifer Serravallo
New York Times Bestselling author and literacy expert

"I have been reading and learning about children's literature and its use in the classroom for decades, and I have never encountered a book as truly transformational as *Judging a Book By More than Its Cover*. Dr. Jiménez goes beyond the surface of children's literature, inviting readers to engage in deep, critical analysis. She asks us to reflect on our own identities, our own reading lives and our own learning in order to analyze books more thoughtfully. Throughout the book, she brilliantly guides us using her own expertise alongside the insights and resources of others. And she does all of this with honesty, humor and respect for where we might be in our journeys. Most importantly, she helps us learn how to choose books with intention, empowering us to do our very best for the children and families we serve."

—Franki Sibberson
***author of* In Community With Readers: Transforming Reading Instruction with Read-Alouds and Minilessons**

Judging a Book By More Than Its Cover

Judging a Book By More Than Its Cover

A Critical Guide to Choosing Children's Literature

LAURA M. JIMÉNEZ, PhD

Routledge
Taylor & Francis Group
NEW YORK AND LONDON
A Stenhouse Book

Cover art by Siobhan Grady

First published 2027
by Routledge
605 Third Avenue, New York, NY 10158

and by Routledge
4 Park Square, Milton Park, Abingdon, Oxon, OX14 4RN

Routledge is an imprint of the Taylor & Francis Group, an informa business

For Product Safety Concerns and Information please contact our EU representative GPSR@taylorandfrancis.com. Taylor & Francis Verlag GmbH, Kaufingerstraße 24, 80331 München, Germany.

ISBN: 9781032912783 (pbk)
ISBN: 9781003582281 (ebk)

DOI: 10.4324/9781003582281

Typeset in Adobe Text Pro
by KnowledgeWorks Global Ltd.

Access additional online resources and examples by scanning the QR codes or visit www.routledge.com/9781032912783

For Dr. Debbie Reese, Nambé Pueblo, who has tirelessly modeled critical engagement with children's literature for decades. Your American Indians in Children's Literature *has changed the field. I am lucky to have known you as a colleague and a friend.*

CONTENTS

ACKNOWLEDGMENTS

I'd like to thank the scholars who have helped shape this work, including but not limited to Rudine Sims Bishop, bell hooks, Gloria Anzaldúa, and Kimberlé Crenshaw who continue to teach me how to do the important work of bringing critical theory that names systems of power and privilege to the children's literature field.

I also want to thank my peers who bring a fierceness and resolve mixed with raucous laughter and joy to the hard work of changing oppressive practices in classrooms.

And, the authors!

How do I thank the authors that spend countless hours writing, re-writing, avoiding writing, and somehow run the gauntlet of publishing to get what is in their heads onto the page? Those people who just keep bringing stories where kids can recognize themselves and their families within the pages.

Oh, and the author/illustrators ... how do you even DO that? I suspect you have many, many people living in your body to be able to pull off both great narratives and exciting illustrations.

I also need to thank my editor, Kassia Omohundro Wedekind, who convinced me I had something to say.

Most of all, I want to thank my loving partner Leslie and our two wildly wonderful sons, Jake and Alex, for putting up with me all these years.

CHAPTER 1

AN INTRODUCTION TO CHILDREN'S LITERATURE IN EDUCATION

I want to believe Dr. Martin Luther King Jr.'s words that he spoke in his "Remaining Awake Through a Great Revolution" speech (1968): "the arc of the moral universe is long but it bends toward justice." I saw his words when I adopted our sons, when I finally had the right to marry my life partner, when I saw Obama take to the White House, and when I saw the Nassau County School District admit that *And Tango Makes Three* (2005) is not obscene.

And, I also know Newton's first law to be true in our universe: a body in motion will continue in motion with the same speed and direction unless acted upon by an unbalanced force. In other words, change is possible but it takes energy, community, and knowledge.

As you read this book, please know that change always faces resistance, sometimes from within, most often from outside. The good news is now you have a middle-aged, white-presenting Latina lesbian with an unconventional education history, and a complete potty mouth on your side. I am here in these pages urging you forward into action, resistance, and joy.

What could possibly go wrong?

EMPATHY HOARDING IS NOT EMPATHY

Deep inside our brains there is a ton of stuff going on just below our consciousness that deeply affects our everyday lives. One of those things is how we perceive others. We perceive people as part of "*us*"—our community, our people, our family. Or, we perceive people as "*them*"—outsiders, threats, the unknown, and the exotic.

For those who we recognize as part of "*us*" we share resources such as food, shelter, time, and empathy.

But, when we label someone as "*them*", well, they might as well fall in a deep hole and die. They are nothing but a threat to "*us*", to our resources, our knowledge, our very existence.

How do we make these distinctions between "*us*" and "*them*"? There are loads of complicated and startling pieces of research from sociology, psychology, political science, and anthropology all taking on the task of explaining how we perceive others and ourselves. On the most basic level we often perceive people that fall into the "*us*" category as folks who we recognize as being similar and familiar. They look like us, they act like us, they remind us of ourselves. This recognition is often centered around our perceptions of race, gender, sexual identity, class, ability, and a host of other identity markers. In other words, people who we recognize as part of "*us*" are deemed worthy of protection, care, love, and resources. They are fully human, and they are our responsibility.

> How do we make these distinctions between "*us*" and "*them*"?

The good news is there is plenty of evidence that we can expand our perception of "*us*" to include a variety of people who may not traditionally fall within our basic empathy borders. We can recognize the humanity of folks who don't look like us, who don't sound like us, who seem to have very little in common with us, and we can see them as valuable and worthy of inclusion, protection, and love. It takes effort to see our biases and assumptions and to notice when we act on those perceptions and impulses. It takes energy and awareness to change.

But you aren't in this alone. There are lots of folks across the country trying to change the ways we educate children in order to build a more just and inclusive society. We are trying to create spaces for educators to learn and grow and push that arc toward an inclusive and humanizing experience for students. Together, we are going to explore this amazing world of children's literature and, hopefully, develop tools you can put into practice in your classroom.

SO MUCH MORE THAN MERE OBJECTS

Books are amazing. They are magic, science, history, and the future all wrapped up and bound for our consumption. They contain thoughts and feelings from yesterday or from 1,000 years ago that we still have access to today. And, most importantly, books help us see ourselves into the future.

I study children's books from a different perspective than most of my colleagues. I came late to reading—I was about eleven—and there weren't a lot of children's books in my early years, so I sort of skipped over children's literature. In many ways I am very much *unlike* my peers in academia and education. I wasn't a good student. I didn't experience success or comfort or belonging in the classroom, and I certainly didn't see myself in any of the books I was assigned to read in school. I eventually figured out how to wedge myself into the stories that were available to me, but it wasn't easy, and it mostly left bits and pieces of me out, exposed, raw, and chapped.

And let's be clear, I hardly read anything I was assigned in school. Like many students in many ELA classes, I spent more time and energy avoiding the literature assigned in class—the very thought of reading one more book about a white boy and his damn dead dog gave me a cramp. By the time I got to middle school I could not muster enough feigned interest to slog through *Romeo and Juliet* (1597), *The Outsiders* (1967), *The Lion, the Witch and the Wardrobe* (1950), or even *A Wrinkle in Time* (1962). Instead, I was busy visiting the library and reading smut like *Lady Chatterley's Lover* (1927) by D.H. Lawrence and *Forever* (1975) by Judy Blume. I read and reread *The Color Purple* (1982) by Alice Walker because ⋘*lesbians*⋙. I wasn't trying to get smarter, I was trying to figure my way into a world that had no room for a young girl who was resoundingly on the margins of every community. Unsurprising, I wouldn't see myself in a book until I was forty-nine years old when I read Gabby Rivera's *Juliet Takes a Breath* (2016). That experience of not seeing oneself in books is not unique—instead, it is the norm for folks with multiple marginalized identities. How did it take so long to get something like *Juliet Takes a Breath* to get written and published? And, even though this book is consistently banned and challenged—along with almost everything else Gabby Rivera writes—I'm incredibly glad it exists in the world and that I have the privilege to share it and many other great works with the teachers who attend my classes.

I think it is helpful to know how these beautiful and beastly things we call books get made. They are not grown, they are not natural, although there is a life cycle to them. But, like so much else in our world, there is a system at work that was never meant to support or even recognize marginalized communities.

BOOKS IN SCHOOL

I think, like a lot of people, the only image I had of publishing growing up and well into my adult years came from the movies.

There I learned that authors are long suffering, lonely, desperate people who can't write, and, at the same time, can't not write. They are mostly alcoholic, womanizing men with father issues and rumpled clothes. Publishers, on the other hand, are more like Parker Posey in *You've Got Mail,* and Sandra Bullock in *The Proposal.* These women, based on the excellent source material of the movies, were all located in NYC, and were all hard-driving workaholics, in large-rimmed glasses and five-inch heels.

In other words, most people have no idea how books travel from an idea that's an unreachable itch rolling around an author's subconscious, to the $25 object that gets delivered to your door along with doggy treats and that cute t-shirt with a manatee on it. I hate to break it to you, but after tons of research, reading books and watching movies about the publishing industry, I have found the ugly truth ...

Publishing is a business.

That's it. Publishers are not in the business of making the world a better place or creating a better citizenry or fixing the ills of the nation. Publishing is a system with traditions that run alongside technical innovations, commerce, and social expectations. I am not a publisher, nor have I ever worked in the industry—but I have come to understand aspects of the process that help ground my thinking about the kind of children's literature that is available for the classroom.

Children's book publishing is, in some ways, unique among other parts of the field. In kidlit, the intended audience—children—is not the one with the purchasing power. And, yet, the issue of power is going to come up again and again in relation to children's literature. Systematic power is often unseen and evasive, and can only be disrupted by being named and understood. To better understand the relationship between children—who are the end consumers—and the books they read in school I want you to imagine a scenario where you go to a restaurant for dinner.

Children's book publishing is, in some ways, unique among other parts of the field.

Oh, wait, it's 2pm and you aren't hungry.

Doesn't matter.

The restaurant decided when you should eat, so there you are, eating dinner when you are not hungry. To add insult to injury, they don't give you a menu. Instead, the waiter immediately puts down in front of you a beet salad with goat cheese, anemic grilled whitefish with some gooey brown rice and quinoa medley, and a glass of Clamato[1] with no ice.

That's it. That's your meal. Do you like fish? Doesn't matter. Do you even know what quinoa is? No one cares. Don't know what Clamato is? Consider yourself lucky and drink it anyway. Lactose intolerant? You are responsible for working around the cheese and dealing with the aftermath (and, no, we are not going to restock the bathroom). How does that sound?

That is how students are treated in traditional ELA (English Language Arts) classroom curriculum. No one asks students what they want to read, what they are curious about, what they don't want, or what

1 Clamato is tomato juice with a hint of clam broth and other spices. Yes, CLAM broth.

they understand. Before you start hollering about 'not all teachers', I 100 percent agree. Not all teachers are problematic. Some individual teachers, schools, and districts create or modify curriculum to align with humanizing ideals for education. These people and places do exist. But still, what we are talking about are individuals acting within a toxic system of education.

Perhaps we are experiencing the result of colliding storms; the overwhelming whiteness of children's literature, the overwhelming whiteness of educators, the overwhelming whiteness of publishing and curriculum companies, along with the overwhelming reliance on packaged curriculum such as *Into Reading* and *Journeys* by Houghton Mifflin Harcourt, Fountas & Pinnell's *Leveled Literacy Intervention* and *Wit & Wisdom* by Great Minds. This collision has resulted in the continuation of a whitening of the American education system.

An in-depth analysis of children's books in K-8 curricula completed in 2023 by the Education Trust Organization illustrates the issues with a few key findings, not only regarding the underrepresentation of non-white characters, but perhaps more importantly, the quality of those characters. "When people of color are included in curricula, they are often portrayed in limited ways. Almost half of the people of color centered in the books we read are one-dimensional, portrayed negatively, or do not have agency" (Marshall and Rodick 2023, 5). As such, even when teachers attempt to diverge from or disrupt the systemic issues of power and privilege in the ELA curriculum, there aren't a lot of resources to support them.

Instead, the people with the money—many levels of adults in various gatekeeping positions like curriculum designers and publishers, policy makers, law makers, and even teachers, in some instances—have the power. And, these gatekeepers are often at odds with the actual readers. Adults want *literature* (said with the worst fake-posh English accent) that fulfills some unsaid, unexplained, completely unexamined expectations. What students often end up with are books that are part of an official or unspoken educational canon, leading to students today being assigned about 80 percent of the same books I was assigned back in the 1980s. And much of that literature was racist, sexist, ableist, and homophobic then, as it still is today.

The crime of it all is that there has been a veritable renaissance in children's literature. In recent years, some publishers have seen fit to recognize an untapped and motivated market of parents, librarians, and teachers who have turned Dr. Rudine Sims Bishop's scholarship into a banner held high proclaiming: **Children deserve to see themselves and to learn about others within the literature they read in school! Know better and do better. Rich, diverse literature in the classroom!**

As you may already know, picture books in particular are works of art that you can take home with you. They are no longer just tools to convey moral lessons; instead, they are places to wander, to explore over and over, to get lost in, and to truly appreciate the emotional impact and power of the images within them. There are early readers and middle grade books that are so much more than training manuals for assimilation into a racist, sexist, ableist, and homophobic society; they feature complex characters who are all kinds of complicated and messy. And, the absolute explosion in recent years of graphic novels for young readers is something entirely unseen before; these graphic novels make authentic stories inclusive and accessible for a wide variety of readers. And still, there are far too few books that represent marginalized communities with respect, knowledge, and love.

And it matters. Just as the disability rights activists insist "Nothing About Us Without Us", it is paramount that stories about marginalized people should come from within our communities. Lee & Low, the largest multicultural publishing house, is at the forefront of representation in children's literature. They are not only in the business of creating and distributing children's books that represent marginalized communities, but they are also invested in research about publishing. In 2013, 2018, and most recently in 2021, Lee & Low collaborated with University of Wisconsin's Cooperative Children's Book Center (CCBC) to create an infographic that clearly illustrates something they refer to as the "by and/or about phenomenon" in children's books (Figure 1.1). In this work, "diverse" was defined as racially non-white which included Black, Indigenous, People of Color (BIPOC) authors and characters.

I want to note here that although these data are focused on race, marginalization includes race, gender, sexual orientation, disability, religion,

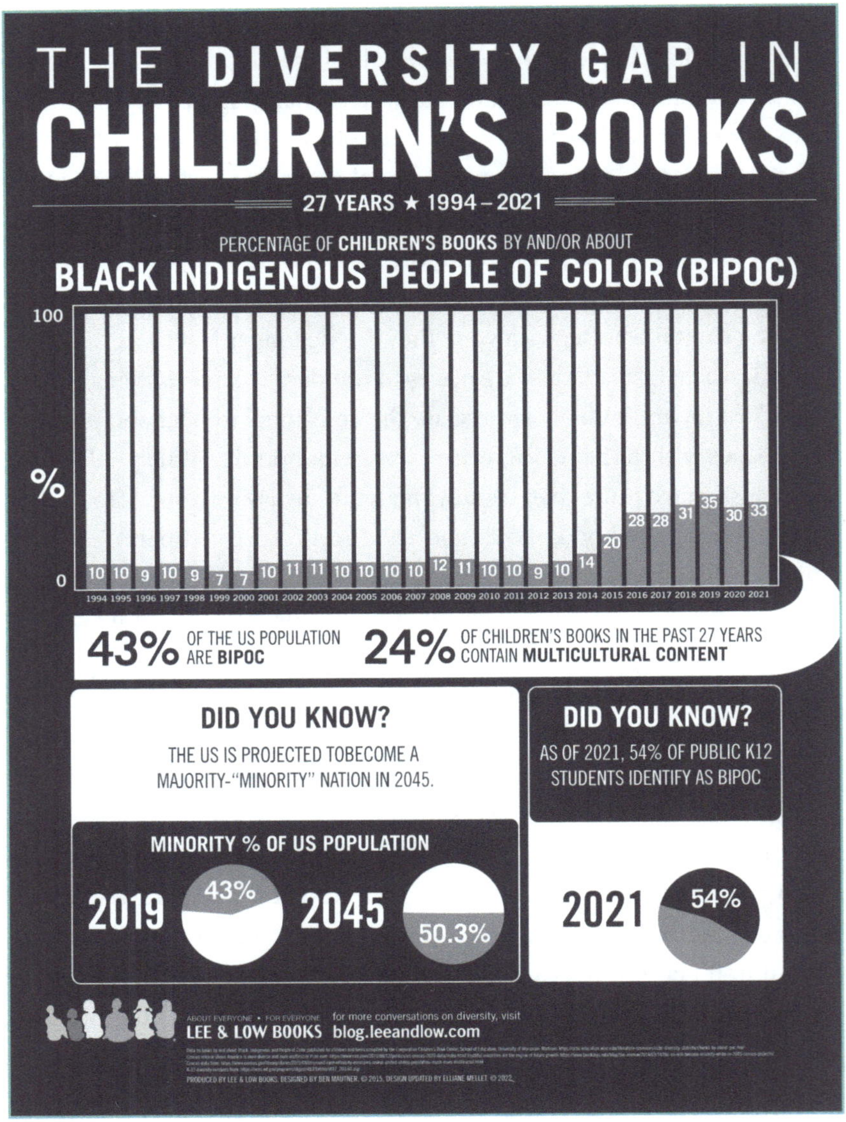

FIGURE 1.1

The Diversity Gap in Children's Books

language, and class. These identities are all working together at all times. We will dig into marginalized identities throughout this book, so get ready.

As you can see in Figure 1.1, children's books written by or about BIPOC authors and characters hovered between 7–12 percent for almost twenty years (1994–2013). Then, in 2014, there was a slight rise to 14 percent that marked the beginning of a steady upward trend. When we look at this kind of data it's important to contextualize the change. What was happening in the US in 2014? What could have been some of the contributing factors that led to this change in children's and young adult (YA) publishing? Around this time:

- Midterm elections in 2014 saw a Republican take-over of the senate
- The ALS ice bucket challenge was in full swing on social media
- Obama was in the middle of his second term as president
- In August 2014, Darren Wilson, a white police officer, fatally shot and killed an unarmed Michael Brown, a Black teen in Ferguson, Missouri, leading to weeks of protests
- And, 2014 saw the beginning of a movement within publishing: #WeNeedDiverseBooks. Ellen Oh and Malinda Lo began a conversation on Twitter about the overabundance of white, male authors in children's and YA literature. Not just the over representation, but the assumption in publishing that readers only wanted to buy books authored by white men. The hashtag led to the formation of the nonprofit We Need Diverse Books (WNDB) that is involved in promoting diversity in kidlit publishing

In the backdrop of the national conversation focused on systemic racial violence, the rise of the Republican senate, as well as the historic Obama presidency, 2014 saw the beginning upward trend of books that are by or about BIPOC characters.

It's important to note that while the percentage of children's books "by and/or about" BIPOC began to increase in 2014, the category of "by and/or about BIPOC" itself is a fairly broad catch-all of children's books that are either authored *by*, or are *about* People of Color, Native, or Black folks. The category includes books by white authors that feature Black, Asian, Native, or Latine characters. The data also includes books written by Black, Indigenous, and People of Color that only feature white or anthropomorphized characters. We have to keep in mind that this data is a reflection of the number of non-white representations and authors, not the quality of the works. When we look at data, we must be clear about what the data is and is not showing.

In 2024 the CCBC reported that a substantial number of books (around 49 percent) feature what they refer to as significant BIPOC content, defined as "a primary or significant secondary character or human subject who is BIPOC, or the setting or topic of the book relates to BIPOC people or history" (Dickinson 2024). And yet, we have to temper that good news with an understanding of what we are seeing and what we are not seeing. We don't see if these books that feature "BIPOC people or history" are actually written by the people in those communities. Again, the data collected were solely focused on the *quantity* of representation and do not contribute to our understanding of the *quality* of those representations. We don't see if these representations are across multiple marginalized communities or one or two. And, perhaps most importantly for our purposes, we don't know if and how these books are being used in classrooms or curricula with actual students.

That is where your knowledge comes in. Teachers need to learn to locate and evaluate literature that is new and falls outside their own experiences, identities, and understanding of the world. Educators might need to let go of some of their favorite, most cherished, and most reliable books for the classroom. All I can say is, for me, a book is an object, and objects will never be more important than people. I want students to have the experience of getting totally absorbed in a book, to be exuberantly exhausted when it ends, to be expectant when they learn it is part of a series, and to be haunted by the ghosts of characters that touched their hearts. That experience does not need to come from the same book I read or enjoyed as a young person because this isn't about me. The books that made me who I am cannot be taken away—in fact I reread books that were important to me as a teen all the time. Those experiences cannot be taken from me or from you. And, at the very same time, when it comes to the books we choose to read and offer children in the classroom, we can leave some of those books in our past. We can do better. We have better. We, as the adults in the room, have got to let go of our nostalgia.

Teachers need to learn to locate and evaluate literature that is new and falls outside their own experiences, identities, and understanding of the world.

HOW THIS BOOK WORKS

When I was first mapping out this book I couldn't figure out how I was going to communicate the kind of dynamic, reactive, flexible classroom I try to achieve when teaching undergrad and graduate students. I often think about the content in three ways:

1. The first level of content—found in the Didja Know? sections—is the stuff that just sort of needs to be learned and you may or may not know. Things like the vocabulary we use to talk about picture books, issues of representation that are based in history or data, and concepts such as genre conventions and narrative structures. This is the summative knowledge that helps ground people's understanding of children's and YA literature

2. The next level of content is designed to have you, the reader, actively reflect on your own experiences, knowledge, and assumptions around children's literature. In this book you'll see spaces for you to take notes or make lists, especially in the beginning chapters. This notetaking and reflection process helps make your thinking and feelings much more concrete and will help you start the habit of reflecting on your language, your own history, and your unchallenged assumptions

3. The last level of content is the hardest and most likely to cause you to throw this book across the room in disgust. I see my role as a guide to how power and privilege is often overlooked and unnoticed to those who are in proximity to it. I'll shine light on things in children's literature you may not have ever noticed and, like any good tour guide, I'll tell you the history or the reason behind that thing that you never noticed. My hope is once you see the ways power and privilege warp the education system (including how we choose and utilize children's literature in the classroom) you won't be able to take your eyes off of it. After that, you'll notice all the ways the system resists change, and, ideally, you'll use what you learn here and the resources that are recommended to you, and act as a force for change

There aren't a lot of right or wrong answers in this book. That isn't the kind of thinking I am asking you to practice. Instead, I'm asking you to do the hard work of considering ideas and phenomena that may paint your teaching practices in less than stellar ways. This is the work that asks you to notice and grapple with ideas you hold dear without thought or reason, move toward change, and, hopefully, enjoy the journey. Let's dive into the wonderful world of judging a book by more than its cover.

DIDJA KNOW?

HANDY HABITS FOR RECOGNIZING REPRESENTATION IN CHILDREN'S LITERATURE

Welcome to the first Didja Know? of this book. These are short chapterettes designed to provide knowledge—technical, historical, industry focused—that help round out the way you think of children's literature. These short chapters also give us a common language to talk through more complex ideas. Consider this first Didja Know? to be a bit of a primer on representation in children's literature and some tools and exercises we can use to help us consider representation as we choose books for the classroom.

Look, no one can change an issue they don't recognize. And there are lots of issues to recognize around the ways marginalized people are represented in books, including but not limited to erasure, tokenism, stereotyping, and general misrepresentation. The quality of the representation in children's books is incredibly important, but the fact that so many marginalized groups are simply erased or tokenized in books is something we have to notice, name, and push against.

Look, no one can change an issue they don't recognize.

For example, if you and your own family look similar to the ones often represented in most picture books (cis, white, straight, middle class,

Christian, English-speaking) you might not immediately recognize the deserts of representation of folks outside those identities. And let me be 100 percent clear, I am not even addressing the authenticity of such representation. I am just talking about the occurrence of seeing characters that reflect marginalized identities. In other words, this is a super low bar. Like, an under the floorboards kind of bar.

I sometimes have education students look at how the representation of marginalized groups has changed over time in children's books and say, "but what about the white authors that can't get published because of this?" pointing at Lee & Low's infographic (Figure 1.1). And I get it, when privilege gets pushed, it pushes back. We have had so many years of historic overrepresentation of cis, white, male characters that seeing anything else can feel odd, like wearing someone else's pants to go and get the mail. The pants might do the same work but it *feels* strange.

> The best news is that the more you practice taking a critical lens, the more the absence of diverse representations of communities will stand out to you.

The best news is that the more you practice taking a critical lens, the more the absence of diverse representations of communities will stand out to you. If you are new to this idea, Table 1 highlights some time-honored classics that are popular because they are comfortable and familiar, but that also reflect racist, sexist, misogynistic, ableist stereotypes. These books are ones that teachers, librarians, and parents love because they don't recognize the representation as problematic because ... well, it's either not a problem for them, they haven't actually read the book as an adult, or (my personal fave) they are nostalgic and can't see the book beyond their own feelings.

TABLE 1

A SELECTION OF POPULAR AND PROBLEMATIC CHILDREN'S BOOKS	
The Rainbow Fish (1992) by Marcus Pfister	This beloved picture book (which also has a board book version for the youngest of readers) tells the tale of a fish with rainbow-colored scales who is seen as a big show off because of these scales. In order to fit in, the rainbow fish rips off their scales and distributes them to the other fish so everyone can share the rainbow fish's color. In other words, being different is so bad, you are better off maiming yourself to fit in. (More on *The Rainbow Fish* in Chapter 3.)
***Skippyjon Jones* series** (2003) by Judy Schachner	This series of picture books centers on a Siamese cat family with an unruly son, Skippyjon Jones, who gets sent to his room when he's in trouble, goes into his closet, and pops out into a magical land called sort-of-like-Mexico-or-the-desert-somewhere-on-the-border. Using fake Spanish as the butt of jokes, this book perpetuates racist stereotypes of Latine folks as lazy party animals. Literal animals, as in partying chihuahuas.
A Fine Dessert (2015) written by Emily Jenkins and illustrated by Sophie Blackall	This picture book represents an enslaved woman as a cook, as well as enslaved children serving white owners with peaceful acceptance. At one point the enslaved woman and an enslaved young girl hide in a kitchen cupboard and lick a bowl furtively. The text reads, "Mmmmmm. Mmmmmm. Mmmmmm. What a fine dessert." The book includes no reflection on the fact that enslavement was even happening.
Charlie and the Chocolate Factory (1964) by Roald Dahl	I'm just going to say this once. The Oompa-Loompas in *Charlie and the Chocolate Factory* are originally described by Dahl as "dark-skinned, African pygmies" and are shipped in crates from "Africa" (the entire continent???) to England, kept in the factory to work all the time, and are paid in cocoa pods. In 1973 Dahl revised the depiction after being called out by the NAACP.

Wonder (2012) by R.J. Palacio	In this novel the protagonist, Auggie, is physically disabled. The book follows him, his family, and some classmates as he endures his first year of school. The book vacillates between presenting Auggie as a Frankenstein-esque monster and as a Jesus-like savior who makes abled people better by simply existing beside them. And then he gets an award.
The Indian in the Cupboard (1980) by Lynne Reid Banks	Published in 1980, this novel still graces many classroom and library shelves today. A toy Native dude named Little Bear comes to life, is owned by a white kid, speaks in pretend-Indian broken English and ... it's just awful. Just no.

A COUPLE OF DEFINITIONS

To fully dig into issues of representation in children's books, it is important that we move forward with some shared understanding of the vocabulary that appears throughout this book.

Representation—the ways that communities, individuals, and historical events are depicted. In children's literature, representation includes characters, settings, and narratives. It is important for us to notice and name the ways that stereotypical messages are either reified or disrupted in the children's literature we read. Let's take a look at a few examples of powerful and authentic representation (Table 2).

TABLE 2

TITLE/AUTHOR/ ILLUSTRATOR	REPRESENTATION
My Colors, My World/Mis colores, mi mundo (2007) Written and illustrated by Maya Gonzalez	In this picture book, a little Latine girl lives in the desert, which she loves, but one day her world is covered in a layer of sandy dust. She misses the colorful world. Her friends help her find the colors again from bright purples, deep greens, and shiny blacks. She uncovers what was always there and shares the beauty with us. This picture book is a great alternative to *The Rainbow Fish*.

The Proudest Blue: A Story of Hijab and Family (2019) Written by Ibtihaj Muhammad with S.K. Ali (both authors are Muslim women who wear hijab) and illustrated by Hatem Aly	This picture book tells the story of an older sister's first day wearing her hijab to school, told from her younger sister's point of view. Hatem Aly's beautiful illustrations help convey some of the complex emotions this little girl is navigating. This short text includes representation of Muslim girls, the realities of wearing hijab, and naming/disrupting Islamophobia.
Fry Bread: A Native American Family Story (2019) Written by Kevin Noble Maillard (an enrolled citizen of the Seminole) and illustrated by Juana Martinez-Neal (a Peruvian-born woman)	This picture book is a depiction of a modern-day Indigenous family sharing a traditional meal. The end papers, captioned "We are still here", name hundreds of Indigenous nations, tribes, and bands—both federally recognized and not.
Mr. Watson's Chickens (2021) Written by Jarrett Dapier (a cis, white, man), illustrated by Andrea Tsurumi (Japanese and Jewish, uses they/them pronouns)	A gay couple and some chickens—what could possibly go wrong? In this picture book Mr. Watson loves chickens and Mr. Nelson loves Mr. Watson and somehow they end up with 456 chickens taking over their home and their small town. The book is gentle and funny, full of motion and excitement and love.

#OwnVoices—books by and about marginalized people. The folks writing (or illustrating) the story are part of the marginalized community represented in the book. (More on #OwnVoices in Chapter 2.) Almost all of the books I teach with are #OwnVoices (either author or illustrator or both). These books don't have to be issue books—where the problem or narrative tension is caused by the marginalized identity—but for some books those issues might be at the center. What is important is that the people telling the story are from within that community. #OwnVoices doesn't guarantee the quality of the representation. Instead it is one factor among many that contributes to broadening the representation of marginalized communities in children's literature. Table 3 highlights just a few of my favorite #OwnVoices children's books.

TABLE 3

A FEW FAVORITE #OWNVOICES CHILDREN'S BOOKS	
TITLE/AUTHOR/ ILLUSTRATOR	**REPRESENTATION**
¡Vamos! Let's Go to the Market (2019) (*World of ¡Vamos!* series) Written and illustrated by Raúl the Third (a Mexican-American) and colors by Elaine Bay (a white woman)	The entire series, like much of Raúl the Third's other work, features culturally appropriate anthropomorphized animals shopping, working, and enjoying the Mercado.
The Gate, The Girl, and the Dragon (2025) Written and illustrated by Grace Lin (a Taiwanese American woman)	In this middle grade novel, Jin, a stone lion Gongshi (guardian) accidentally closes the portal between our world and the spirit world. He must accept help from a Lulu (a tween girl), and a worm (who might be a tiny dragon) to reopen the gate. The story highlights Chinese folklore within a contemporary adventure story.
I Talk Like a River (2020) Written by Jordan Scott (who speaks with a stutter) and illustrated by Sydney Smith	This picture book tells the author's own story. As a child with a profound stutter, he felt isolated much of the time. This book shows one rather unremarkable day in his life, when he and his father walk by a river to enjoy each other's company and find some peace. This is both an #OwnVoices book as well as an issue book. The narrative tension centers on the young boy who stutters, making communication difficult. The solution is not that he is rid of his stutter, but instead the resolution is that he and his father connect.

DEVELOP A HABIT OF NOTICING

We can become more adept at noticing issues of representation if we build a purposeful habit of mind, especially if we are either new to this work or if we are woefully underprepared and overprivileged. No shame—just facts. For example, I might be well-versed in noticing when characters who share my own marginalized identities are missing, but it means work for me to see those issues of representation and erasure that are outside my personal knowledge. Also, it has taken work for me to recognize, name, and not accept the more insidious and biased gender roles that children's literature is overflowing with. Each one of us has some kinds of deeply ingrained and unrecognized biases and privileges because we are the product of our society.

The Bechdel-Wallace Test: A Tool for Noticing

Probably the most versatile tool we can use to analyze issues of representation in media was originally illustrated by Alison Bechdel in her weekly comic strip *Dykes to Watch Out For.* The strip ran for twenty-five years (1983–2008) in LGBTQIA+ newspapers around the country. It was one of the earliest representations of lesbians in media that showed all the positive, endearing, multi-faceted, complex, and messy ways our community functions. One particular strip called "The Rule" outlined a conversation Bechdel had with her friend Liz Wallace about creating some sort of scale or warning about women's representation in movies. "The Rule" was later picked up and built upon by Anita Sarkeesian, founder of the now-closed *Feminist Frequencies,* a website focused on the representation of women in pop culture media. She used "The Rule" as a way to look closely at who was represented in movies, television, and video games.

Think about a movie or book you have recently watched or read and think about if:

- There are two named women, *who*
- talk to each other, *about*
- something besides a man.

That's it. That's all. Nothing else.

The Bechdel-Wallace Test is simply a tool to help you notice the most basic, low bar, simplest aspect of representation in media. It has nothing to do with the quality of the representation. It is simply a way to recognize who is there on the page or screen. After all, you can't start to even deal with the misrepresentation of a community if that community is wholly missing.

So many books, especially those most read in schools, do *not* pass the Bechdel-Wallace Test. Think about texts like *The Great Gatsby* (1925), *Of Mice and Men* (1937), *Romeo and Juliet* (1597). The list is extensive. More recent books, and books written by women, tend to be more likely to pass the test. Books like *The Help* (2009), *To Kill a Mockingbird* (1960), *Beloved* (1987) all have multiple, named female-identified characters that have conversations about things other than men and so they all pass, when we restrict the representation to women.

But, what about using the same basic set of rules to look at other marginalized groups? Rules like:

- There are two named Black people, *who*
- talk to each other, *about*
- something besides *white people* or *whiteness*

If we start looking at this—a whole lot of those books will drop off. *The Help*, a novel by Kathryn Stockett, a white woman, has multiple named Black characters, and, in fact, has an abundance of Black women characters that talk to each other. But, they are solely interested in the ways white people, whiteness, and white supremacy affects them. In my experience, marginalized folks have other things to deal with, think about, talk about, and act upon other than all the privileged identities they interact with.

You can use any *marginalized* identity in the Bechdel-Wallace Test to get an idea of who is represented. All too often marginalized characters are used to signal the presence of "diversity" but really, these characters are there to promote, fix, and support the privileged characters. Here are some examples to try out on your own:

two named LGBTQIA+ folks, *who* talk to each other, *about* something besides *straight people*	two named lesbians, *who* talk to each other, *about* something besides *straight women*	two named gay men, *who* talk to each other, *about* something besides *straight women*
two named Asian characters, *who* talk to each other, *about* something besides *whiteness*	two named Latine characters, *who* talk to each other, *about* something besides *whiteness*	two named Indigenous characters (including tribal affiliation), *who* talk to each other, *about* something besides *whiteness*
two named disabled characters, *who* talk to each other, *about* something besides *ability*		

The DuVernay Test (Massie 2016) is more nuanced compared to the Bechdel-Wallace Test, therefore it often uncovers the more difficult to identify kinds of characteristics of books that may appear to be fabulous but turn out to be trash once you scratch the surface. Let's explore the DuVernay Test by looking at two children's books that focus on racial identity and community for young children. Both books aim to provide a view of a racially diverse and cooperative world.

Let's start with *The World Needs More Purple Schools* (2022) written by Kristen Bell and Benjamin Hart and illustrated by Daniel Wiseman. In this book—one in a series of "purple world" picture books—Bell features a white girl named Penny Purple who lives in a world where all the ills are fixed by "mixing red and blue" to create a purple world. Once the school is painted purple, then all that the kids, teachers, and community members need to do is "roll your sleeves up and work really hard". In other words, we are all better off if we ignore the differences among us. The myth of meritocracy where everyone can attain anything by working is alive and well, and there are no impediments to BIPOC and LGBTQIA+ or disabled people to "just be you".

Lots of white teachers flocked to this series because it avoided conflict and responsibility and provided a simple (if completely illogical and ridiculous) solution to real issues of harm and trauma. These books completely simplify and erase hundreds of years of systematic racism, ableism, sexism, and homophobia. Unsurprisingly, the series is created by three cis, straight, abled, white people.

And so, it completely fails the DuVernay Test:

- Feature at least two characters of color? YES
- They must not be in a romantic relationship together? YES
- Characters of color must have complex lives rather than existing only in relation to white characters. ABSO-FREAKING-LUTELY NOT! Not even a little bit.

In *The World Needs More Purple Schools*, middle class white civility is the absolute unquestioned norm against which everything else is measured. It is a white savior's dream of a color-blind society where everyone is the same—instead of everyone being white, everyone is some middle-of-the-road purple. Same idea, different day.

Next, let's look at *The Day You Begin* (2018) written by Jacqueline Woodson and illustrated by Rafael López. In this story Angelina, an Afro Latine girl, is starting school somewhere in America. She has dark skin, and lots and lots of beautiful curly black hair. The kids in her class are racially diverse—Asian, white, Latine, and Black—but none are exactly like her. The class starts talking about what they did during the summer and Angelina feels ashamed because she didn't travel. Instead she spent the summer with her little sister, on their block, reading about all the places in the world. López illustrates her feelings of isolation and vulnerability by showing Angelia sitting, knees drawn up in a sort of protective stance, surrounded by muted greys, while everyone else is standing in a kaleidoscope of color and shapes. *The Day You Begin* further illustrates Angelina's feelings by showing how other classmates also feel excluded at times because of many perceived differences—their language, their food, and their disabilities. Woodson presents a reality in which kids are all kinds of different—each one dealing with the same feelings of being alone. And then, Angelina finds the courage to begin speaking about her summer, opening the door for her classmates to truly see her. López's illustrations help the reader see a change by showing Angelina and a classmate on swings in a world filled with laughter, flowers, and sunlight.

Woodson doesn't place blame or guilt or any kind of judgment on the fact that people are different. And unlike *The World Needs More Purple Schools*, she also does not suggest that being the same is the solution. Instead, the solution to being isolated is to be seen and heard and respected for who you are in the world. Woodson explains it this way ... "every new friend has something a little like you—and something else so fabulously not quite like you at all".

And that's it—*The Day You Begin* gives all of us a model for the ways we should expect our friends to see us for who we are, in all our differences and in all the ways we can explore the world to find each other. I really love great books with gorgeous illustrations and examples of kids being vulnerable and human.

The more we understand issues of representation, the more we develop a practice of noticing who is represented in children's books and how they are represented, the better we will all become at recognizing the amazing books that exist in the world into our classrooms.

CHAPTER 2

STORIES MATTER: HOW POWER AND PRIVILEGE SHOW UP WITHIN CHILDREN'S LITERATURE

There are so many ways books are used in schools: to entertain, to maintain order, to convey information, to create community, to moralize, to illustrate standards and norms, to practice skills, and probably a dozen more ways. I want to focus on the ways we, the adults in the room, think and feel about the stories we use in the classroom because, at the end of the day, the stories we tell (and don't tell) matter. The stories students hear and study reflect the values we—as adults—want to convey, what we want to hide, and how we want children to act in and react to the world.

I want to bring a sense of responsibility and criticality to the choices we make as gatekeepers of children's literature. By and large, adults are the writers, editors, publishers, booksellers, curriculum designers, librarians, teachers, and often readers of the books we bring into the classroom. Last in line are the students and because of that, we have to admit that they—students—have the least power in this discussion.

I want to bring a sense of responsibility and criticality to the choices we make as gatekeepers of children's literature.

Because of this incredible imbalance of power we need to be honest about the choices adults make and the reasons behind those choices. These honest conversations can lead to some uncomfortable realizations, but they can also lead to much needed changes to the ways we recognize the abundance of brilliant and beautiful children's literature that exists.

ADULTS AS CHILD READERS

When I ask most adults—especially teachers and librarians—to talk about books they loved as kids, I often see a wave of nostalgia wash over them like a warm and fuzzy blanket that smells like fresh baked cookies. Most ELA educators and librarians love books and find comfort, confidence, and self-satisfaction in remembering the books that have stayed with us over the years. The books that were read to you, that you read, and the stories that you experienced as a child are important. They meant something to you. Your favorite books often mark stages and events in your life, or important people in your history. These stories that hold emotional memories are valuable to you. These are the stories—for good or ill—that helped make you the person you are today.

Take a moment to think about the books you experienced from an early age. First, what books did you love as a kid that were *not* part of the school curriculum? These are books you read with your caretakers, books you found on your own, books that you selected. Take a moment and list some titles and keep this list handy—we will return to it in a minute.

Books I Loved in the Wild as a Child	

Now, think about the books that were read to you or that were assigned to you to read in school. Think back as early as you can. To do this, first think about where you lived when you were six, seven, and eight years old. Where did you go to school? What did the building look like? Who were your teachers? What did the rooms look like? Who did you sit next to? What did recess look like? Now, write down the titles you remember being assigned to read or books that your teacher read to you.

Books from School	

Lastly, if you are a parent, caregiver, or teacher, list the books you read to your kids, books you assign to your students, or books that the curriculum includes.

Books I Read to Kids or I Assign in School	

Now set these lists aside, we are going to come back to them in a minute.

COMMON AND WELL-LOVED BOOKS FOR CHILDREN

When I ask adults about the books they loved as kids, they often name picture books like the *Berenstain Bears* series (1962), *Clifford the Big Red Dog* (1963), *The Very Hungry Caterpillar* (1969), and *If You Give a Mouse a Cookie* (1985). They also remember authors like Richard Scarry, Leo Lionni, Mercer Mayer, and Dr. Seuss. In general, these books are often remembered as gentle and nice; these books were designed to be simple stories told in a didactic manner to teach a clear and defined lesson or moral. Picture books and early readers are often stories that illustrate, explicitly or implicitly, how to be the "right" kind of person. They also illustrate, sometimes explicitly, but often in the noted absences, what kind of person is not the "right" kind of person, who to fear, who to ignore, and who to belittle.

Novels like *Anne of Green Gables* (1908), *Hatchet* (1987), *Sarah Plain and Tall* (1985), *The Baby-Sitters Club* series (1986), *Ramona the Pest* (1968), and *Cam Jansen* series (1980) often make adults' lists of favorite children's books as well. Depending on the age of respondents, I might also hear about favorite books that range from *A Wrinkle in Time* (1962) to *The Maze Runner* (2009) to *The Chronicles of Narnia* (1950), to *The Phantom Tollbooth* (1961). Although novels often have less of a didactic flavor to them, they still highlight who is and who is not valued, who is worthy of stories being told about them, and most importantly, who has the opportunity to tell stories.

Often (and this is going to hurt a bit) the stories that we grew up with were a product of the society and time they were written, which was, historically, utter trash for marginalized people. I like to think about this the way Roland Barthes did. He was a French literary philosopher and is pretty famous in exceedingly overeducated academic literary circles. He wrote an essay titled "The Death of the Author" (1977) in which he argues that the author brings their entire self—their language, personal history, and beliefs—to the act of writing, and when the pen leaves the paper, the author is dead to the work. At that point, the author and their intentions no longer matter, and the reader takes over to make meaning from the text. This idea opens the possibility for literature—especially children's literature—to be an active and engaging conversation between the reader and the text. But, how can a reader be an active participant when the text is one note, one lesson, one tone, one person?

This should not come as a surprise to you so I'm going to just put it out there. The views and beliefs that are often held by a society are geared to protect and promote the most privileged in that society. In the US context, this means that the books that show up in the classroom most often reflect our society's *idealized norm*—white, male, cis, straight, abled, Christian, English-speaking monolingual, and middle class. This idealized norm is a driving force in most of the systems we create and live within—law, medicine, education, commerce, and media, to name a few. We live in a society with the deeply held (if sometimes subconscious) knowledge that this idealized norm is something we should all strive toward, as if it is an attainable ideal. For those of us who disrupt this ideal by our very existence, the results are dire indeed—loss of earnings, loss of opportunities, and sometimes, loss of life.

And yet, there is hope. As we've already begun to explore, in the last few years there has been a renaissance in children's literature. The number of truly extraordinary picture books, novels, and graphic novels that represent a wide array of communities, stories, and histories is heartening. It isn't enough—how could it be? There are still tremendous gaps in representation but we are headed in the right direction. Except, like all systems, the systems that these books live within (education, media, and commerce) are fighting back. For every step forward in wider representation, there are more book challenges and legal actions designed to repress the stories.

Adult gatekeepers have to decide where they want to position themselves. There is no neutral in this situation. You are either on the side of diversifying children's literature or you are against it. You are either going to push against banning and challenging books or you are going to sit back and support taking these much needed voices out of the hands of students. Don't be fooled, the act of restricting stories and voices directly reflects the need systems have to protect and promote that idealized norm and thus to keep power and privilege tightly controlled by a few hands.

And, the worst part of all of this is that the closer you are to this idealized norm, the harder it is to recognize.

REFLECTING ON REPRESENTATION

Let's get back to those lists you just made. The books you loved as a child, the books you experienced in school, and the books you use now. Is there overlap between your lists? For some people, the list of books you loved and books in school are one and the same. For others, there is little to no crossover between the lists. All of these books represent your literary autobiography—the books you remember as an adult are the ones that stuck with you for many reasons, and the books you still hold onto. Sometimes the books we loved as children are really about the feelings you experienced in those moments; being read to is comforting. Perhaps you remember a trusted adult sharing a favorite book with you and that experience is incredibly rich and important to the person you were then, and the person you grew into today, and the person you will be going forward. The thing is ... this experience often isn't really about the book. It is about the personal connection and the influence on your personhood. The nostalgia you might feel for that book is a heady mixture of text, circumstance, emotional connectedness, and physical sensations that you hold dear to your heart.

And, I do not want to take that from you. Instead, I want you to expand the possibilities for others to share that feeling without the harm that a lot of these books do to marginalized people.

Now, to finish the literary autobiography—write down how you identify. It is very important that you write this down and be as honest as possible. Use the words that represent the you that you feel is the truth. We will start with just a few easy ones:

I identify as (race)— ______________________________

I identify as (gender)— ______________________________

I identify as (sexual orientation)— ______________________

Here are mine—for an example:

I identify as (race)—White-presenting Latina or Chicana

I identify as (gender)—Cis woman

I identify as (sexual orientation)—Long-time lesbian (first-time caller)

Take a few minutes and fill in the table that follows (a reproducible copy is also found in Appendix A). Start with listing some information about the gender, race, and sexual orientation of the protagonists from some of your favorite childhood books, as well as the books you read in school. Use the text and images to make a best guess—after all, that is what we do in real life. We look at someone and decide on their identity. We can always be wrong, but we often use scant evidence to identify people. Lean into it and just guess—no one is going to know. This is only for you.

A Literary Autobiography of Books You Loved as a Child or Read in School

BOOK TITLE	PROTAGONIST'S		
	RACE	GENDER	SEXUAL ORIENTATION

A note: while we have focused here on three important elements of identity—race, gender, and sexual orientation—we could also complete this same exercise considering other elements of identity including ability/disability, religion, socio-economic status, and language.

If stories matter, then the stories of marginalized people matter. The stories of marginalized people, those of us who do not adhere to the idealized norm (reminder—the idealized norm identity is white, abled, cis, middle class, English-speaking, Christian, and male), matter to everyone. If we want to change who is represented in the children's literature that is read in schools and classrooms, then we have to admit our own biases, comfort, and preferences. If you are part of the idealized norm, you have experienced plenty of representation—you have seen yourself represented in the past, present, and future. There is a vast cultural library featuring the idealized norm that you have access to at any given moment. We must ask ourselves and others: Who deserves to be seen in a variety of authentic ways? Why are so many being omitted? Who are we trying to protect and from what are we protecting them from when we deny history and people?

We must ask ourselves and others: Who deserves to be seen in a variety of authentic ways? Why are so many being omitted?

A SPECIAL NOTE ON #OWNVOICES

In 2015, an author, Corinne Duyvis, musing on Twitter, suggested a hashtag, #OwnVoices, to signal a book written by and about "diverse" characters (2015). Duyvis, herself, is on the autism spectrum and her YA novels, including *Otherbound* (2014), *On the Edge of Gone* (2016), and *The Art of Saving the World* (2020), all feature protagonists who are also on the spectrum. In creating the #OwnVoices hashtag, Duyvis was trying to capture the intangible and undeniable element of a book that features marginalized characters that makes it feel true and authentic.

I've spent a lot of my scholarly time trying to identify, quantify, and illustrate what makes a story, a point of view, a character voice, plot line, and setting authentic to marginalized communities. I can't create a rubric or a checklist for that ethereal taste of authenticity, but I can feel it in my bones when it happens. In my own teacher education classes, I only teach with #OwnVoices literature. Although there may be great books out there written by and about white, straight, abled, cis, men and women, they don't need my help. They don't need to be further highlighted or taught. Those books are going to be just fine without me. Instead, I am committed to helping teachers learn to recognize and appreciate books that do *not* center the idealized norm. I want to highlight the books that most white, straight, cis, abled teachers don't automatically relate to because, as readers, they are unused to seeing literature that reveals anything outside the white, straight, abled, cis, experience.

And, I want to be very clear on this point. The fact is that #OwnVoices books are not *automatically* authentic representations of the groups and people they portray. They are not *automatically* unproblematic. Plenty of marginalized people have internalized society's messages and are living with a twisted view of themselves and their community based on a self-hatred that comes out on the pages of their books. Plenty of people from marginalized communities are committed to writing for the dominant gaze. These books adhere to the tropes and expected stereotypes put upon their communities by the larger society—and those stories suffer for it. For example, the picture book *Stonewall: A Building. An Uprising. A Revolution*, written by Rob Sanders and illustrated by Jamey Christoph (2019), white washes and cis washes (not a term but it should be!) the history of the Stonewall uprising. The book gives the gay, white, cis, male community a pat on the back for acts of civil disobedience and disruption that powerful trans women of color, butch women, femme men, and trans men were actually responsible for.

It's important to keep in mind that there is no single book that provides a three-dimensional account of any person, community, or event. Instead, we need to encourage students, and ourselves, to find multiple authentic representations. This is even more important for people who should be centered and are instead often erased. So, instead of a white/cis-washed look at the Stonewall Riots, here are some books to consider that center the voices and experiences of the trans women, butch women, femme men, and trans men who were really at the center of the Stonewall story (Table 4).

It's important to keep in mind that there is no single book that provides a three-dimensional account of any person, community, or event.

This example of a text set (Table 4) accomplishes a few things. First, it provides a look at the event (the Stonewall Riots) from a few points of view. Second, each book is historically accurate. Third, the selection provides

TABLE 4

BOOKS ABOUT THE STONEWALL UPRISING THAT CENTER EXPERIENCES OF TRANS WOMEN, BUTCH WOMEN, FEMME MEN, AND TRANS MEN
Hispanic Star*: *Sylvia Rivera   (2023) written by Claudia Romo Edelman and J. Gia Loving, and illustrated by Cheyne Gallarde   Sylvia Rivera's work did not start, nor end, with Stonewall riots. This picture book helps provide readers with a fuller understanding of Sylvia's lifelong activism with LGBTQIA+ homeless adolescents.
One Day in June: A Story Inspired by the Life and Activism of Marsha P. Johnson   (2025) written by Tourmaline, and illustrated by Charlot Kristensen   This vibrant and love-filled picture book highlights the life of Marsha P. Johnson as she is remembered by her close friends. Johnson's activism and love fill the pages.
The Stonewall Riots: Coming Out in the Streets   (2019) by Gayle E Pitman   Written with older students in mind (grades 6–9), this book provides primary source documents, including interviews, photos, and news reports, about the lead up to the riots.

different readers with opportunities to focus on different aspects of the historical event and people involved in it. As you begin (or continue) to consider issues of power, privilege, and representation in children's literature, #OwnVoices can be one lens you use to consider and choose books for the classroom or your own reading!

FROM THE OUTSIDE LOOKING IN: AUTHORS WHO WRITE OUTSIDE THEIR IDENTITIES AND LIVED EXPERIENCES

And, given all that, #OwnVoices texts are just a starting point. It isn't the only criteria for creating a rich, loving, respectful, and authentic representation of a community. Just as a book that is written by an insider in a community does not guarantee the quality of the representation, there are also rare cases when folks from the dominant community do the work and create representations of marginalized people that are high quality. So, again, by encouraging you to pursue #OwnVoices literature, I am not telling you to totally ignore books written by folks who cross identity lanes. But, what it does mean is that those outsiders to the community have to work harder and they should be aware of their actions and the space they take up within publishing.

One example of someone writing well outside of their own identity or lived experiences is Laurie Halse Anderson, a white, straight, cis woman who wrote the *Chains* YA trilogy (*Chains* (2008); *Forge* (2010); and *Ashes* (2016)). The books are award winning—which, I mean, sure. She's a great writer, so of course she's going to get awards. Anderson is kind of a mystery to me. I don't know if it's a series of personality quirks or professional habits or some random assortment of both that give her the tools and the disposition to write complex representations of Black characters. In the *Chains* trilogy, the protagonist, Isabel, along with her younger sister Ruth, are enslaved young women in New York. *Chains* takes place at the very beginning of the American Revolution and shows the reader the historic events from Isabel's point of view. Isabel narrates both the large political upheavals and the everyday in a way that keeps the reader interested, invested, and engaged. Each book in the trilogy exists within the same world, featuring numerous characters and their intersecting stories. The *Chains* trilogy is a complicated, emotional, difficult, and touching adventure story that gives voice to Black characters that represent many stories. Perhaps most important—and this is an incredibly low bar—at no point in Anderson's books do the white people responsible for the horrors of enslavement get off easy.

As an author, Anderson began her career as a journalist where she developed the tools to research, the habit of asking questions, and the tenacity to spend more time than seems reasonable on that research. But, there is also a curiosity and humility to her writing as well. A sense that the story, the characters, and the events are more important than the author. In fact, in the best sense of the words, the author fades away from the text itself, and the experience that is left is the world created between the reader and the characters. And after all, isn't that what we want in great literature? We want the author to step away and let the story envelope the reader to experience another time, place, and existence.

As you start looking critically at books written by authors "on the outside, looking in", you will want to consider how they are taking steps to authentically represent people.

- Consider how characters from marginalized groups are typically represented in children's books. Are there any problematical, biased or stereotypical representations that give you pause? Are there books you now want to reconsider including in your classroom? (Much, much, much more on this as this book moves forward.)
- Look for book reviews written by people who are members of the groups represented in the children's book
- Make sure you're balancing these "on the outside, looking in"-authored books with books by #OwnVoices authors

HOW DO WE START? CHOOSING DIVERSE CHILDREN'S LITERATURE

Good news! You've already started. You bothered to pick up this book, which indicates you want to learn more about critically engaging with children's literature. So, if you are a list maker, write down "pick up that book about critical kidlit" and check it off so you feel like the path ahead isn't insurmountable. If for you, like me, lists are just promises to be broken, don't bother. Just keep reading.

The next steps are a bit of a let down because the process of engaging critically with children's literature and choosing powerful children's books for the classroom really isn't a checklist kind of thing. Instead, the process is just that—a process. There isn't a defined end, there aren't clean lines of demarcation, and there aren't a lot of right and wrong answers. Instead, you are entering an exciting liminal space filled with the stories of marginalized communities, self-reflection, and growth. As bell hooks wrote, "For me this space of radical openness is a margin – a profound edge" (1989, 19).

Welcome to the edge where the first step is a doozy—begin by reading books, lots of books by and about people you know little about (or what you do know is just plain wrong—we will get to that in a later chapter). The good news is that there are amazing authors and books out there that will push you beyond your childhood favorites to a broader and more beautiful representation of our world. Here are a few ways you can get started:

- **Read books by Indigenous authors** and think about the kinds of background information you, as the teacher, will need to teach that book
    - Explore the work of Dr. Debbie Reese at her website ***American Indians in Children's Literature***. Start at the "best books" tab
    - Find fabulous books at the ***American Indian Library Association***. Go to the awards page and have fun!
- **Read books by Black authors** and think about the kinds of background information you, as the teacher, will need to teach that book
    - Try exploring ***The Brown Bookshelf*** website. They have categories such as PB Bookshelf, MG Bookshelf, and YA Bookshelf to help you locate books for your audience of readers
    - Read books that have won the **Coretta Scott King Award**
- **Read books by Latine authors** and think about the kinds of background information you, as the teacher, will need to teach that book
    - Try ***Latinxs in Kid Lit*** website. Use the "Reviewed Books" tabs to locate picture books, middle grade, and YA
    - Read books that have won the **Pura Belpré Award**

- **And, for extra credit, read books by non-white, LGBTQIA+ authors** and think about the kinds of background information you, as the teacher, will need to teach that book. A few of my favorites to get you started are:
  - *When Aidan Became a Brother* (2019) written by Kyle Lukoff and illustrated by Kaylani Juanita
  - *Kapaemahu* (2022) written by Hinaleimoana Wong-Kalu, Dean Hamer, and Joe Wilson, and illustrated by Daniel Sousa
  - *The Legend of Auntie Po* (2021) by Shing Yin Khor
  - *Hurricane Child (2018)* by Kacen Callender
  - *The Magic Fish* (2020) by Trung Le Nguyen
  - *Last Night at the Telegraph Club* (2021) by Malinda Lo

DIDJA KNOW?
(A BIT OF) THE HISTORY AND ANATOMY OF PICTURE BOOKS

If the first Didja Know? chapterette (page 13) was a primer on representation in children's literature, here we'll take a short tour of picture books as physical objects, how they've changed over time, and how their physical elements contribute to the overall experience of reading them.

A BIT OF PICTURE BOOK HISTORY

Picture books are fairly new to the literary landscape compared to early novels written for adults such as *Pilgrim's Progress* (1678), *Robinson Crusoe* (1719), and *Moll Flanders* (1722).

It's difficult to find a definitive answer on what the very first picture book for children was, but an early popular one was *Der Struwwelpeter* ("shock-headed Peter") (1845), a particularly terrifying text by German author Heinrich Hoffmann (Figure DK.1). This early picture book featured cautionary moral tales of crime and punishment for children.

Early twentieth-century children's literature in Western countries pretty much consisted of either books to get kids to sleep with quiet and repetitive rhythms, like *Goodnight Moon* (1939) by Margaret Wise Brown and *Millions of Cats* (1928) by Wanda Gág or books that served up heavy-handed and didactic moral lessons like most of the Little Golden Books. A few titles in this Golden Book category include:

- *Peter Rabbit* by Beatrix Potter (originally published in England 1902, and later as a Little Golden Book in 1942) is a tale about following rules or becoming rabbit stew

FIGURE DK.1

The cover of *Der Struwwelpeter* (1845) whose terrifying cover image portrays the titular character and the consequences of not taking hygiene seriously.

- *The Poky Little Puppy* (1942) by Janette Sebring Lowrey tells the story of a puppy who is poky (as in a slow poke) and wanders away after repeated warnings, thus missing out on dessert
- *The Three Little Kittens* (originally published in England in 1847, and published in the US as a Little Golden Book in 1944) has a plot that consists of a series of mitten debacles and mother cat's threats that her kittens' naughty behavior might result in them missing out on pie
- *The Little Red Hen* (originally a magazine story in 1874, then published in 1942 as a Little Golden Book) features the story of the heroine hen who works the land to reap the rewards (fresh baked bread) while her fellow farmyard slackers go without

These books were not uniquely American in nature. Many were originally published in Europe and shared many American values such as hard work, perseverance, and thrift. Most of all, these texts provided a road map for the ways we thought (and still think, to a certain extent) children should behave and what they should expect out of life. Picture books in these early days of the form were designed to instruct kids on being good and obedient workers. For loads more information on the history of American children's literature, check out the fabulous article "The Origins and History of American Children's Literature" (2013) by Michael Tunnell and James Jacobs.

The relatively short history of picture books makes sense. After all, children's books are written for kids who famously don't have a lot of disposable income. Additionally, for most of the history of children's books, picture books were intended to serve the utilitarian purpose of training children for adulthood. What's more, most children's books are large physical objects and technologically complicated to print and manufacture, and the readership is likely going to outgrow them quickly and move on. Yet despite the relatively short history of picture books and the fact that

For most of the history of children's books, picture books were intended to serve the utilitarian purpose of training children for adulthood.

there were many fewer children's books available to us as children than there are today, many of us have complex relationships with the books we loved as children.

What is unique about children's literature is the way the books and the reader's experiences of them get tangled together. As readers grow older and move into adulthood, they often become even more fond of the books they read as children. This fondness is folded and stretched by life experiences, molded by the elasticity of memory, and finally becomes nostalgia. The need for literary gatekeepers—parents/caregivers, teachers, librarians—to keep a tight hold on what has become classic or canonical is based on the nostalgia held for books, rather than any kind of realization about the books themselves.

I mean, while literary gatekeepers are clutching their childhood favorites like so many pearls, have you taken a look at picture books lately? There has been an absolute renaissance in just the last twenty years in particular, making picture books the perfect tool for the classroom. As a form (more on this term later) picture books are appropriate for a wide range of ages and can be enormously useful in opening space for complex ideas—everything from teaching mood and tone to point of view, as well as literary devices. They can also be a great way to introduce rarely taught or frequently mistaught historical events in developmentally appropriate ways. One specific example of this is David Robertson and Julie Flett's *When We Were Alone* (2016) which introduces students to the Indian Boarding Schools and the generational trauma that was inflicted by white religious zealots with the support of the government.

THE ANATOMY OF PICTURE BOOKS

Picture books are also immensely flexible—just like any other literary form. Stories can be poignant and heartfelt, they can be funny and irreverent, they can impart lessons or simply entertain. They can be wordless or have swathes of text ready for shared reading. They can be deceptively simple, featuring a single color in the illustrations or full of color popping off the page. They are limitless, but there are a few conventions.

To truly understand the complexity of this form, let's take a close look. I'll need you to grab a picture book published in recent years.

Here are some of my recommendations for this picture book anatomy activity:

- *Drawn Together* (2018) written by Min Lê and illustrated by Dan Santat
- *Love in the Library* (2022) written by Maggie Tokuda-Hall and illustrated by Yas Imamura
- *Fry Bread* (2019) written by Kevin Noble Maillard and illustrated by Juana Martinez Neal

Let's examine the anatomy of picture books, part by part.

CLASSIC PICTURE BOOK STRUCTURE AND DESIGN

Traditionally, most picture books are exactly thirty-two pages long. This has more to do with the printing technology than anything else. There is some amazing paper folding, cutting, printing, rotational axis math going on here that makes thirty-two pages the most economical and efficient way to make a picture book. Still, recent changes in print technology have opened up more possibilities for picture books of different lengths. *Fry Bread* is forty-eight pages long while *Love in the Library* and *Drawn Together* are each forty. (Notice that thirty-two, forty, and forty-eight are all multiples of eight? This isn't a coincidence. Picture books are created by printing on large pieces of paper which are then folded to create eight book pages. Working in multiples of eight is most efficient and cost effective.) Picture books usually do not have page numbers.

BOOK COVERS AND DUST JACKETS

The illustration on the dust jacket of a hardcover picture book often acts as a preview of the story or, at the very least, a clue to the characters and the plot. Take a look at the picture book you chose to examine. First things first ... look to see if the dust jacket illustration matches what is on the book cover underneath. Students are frequently amazed at the fact that the dust cover often illustrates one part of the story and the book cover underneath is completely different!

Take for example, *Drawn Together.* This picture book focuses on a familiar immigrant story. A young boy is dropped off at his grandfather's house and they must share the afternoon together. They are separated by generations, but more importantly perhaps, they are separated by culture and language. At first glance, the dust jacket of this book shows a touching scene between a grandfather and his grandson, surrounded by lively colors and detailed images of the two.

But wait, there's more! Readers are delighted to find that under the dust jacket, there is a plain black cover with the word SKETCH in white block letters. This same image of the plain sketchbook appears later inside the book on a page where the grandson brings out his drawings to pass the time and unexpectedly opens up exciting and active communication between the two characters that bridges age, language, and culture.

PAGE DESIGN

There is nothing accidental or natural about the ways picture books are designed, and the millions of decisions made by a multitude of people mean these books are collaborations involving authors, editors, illustrators, designers, and others. In other words, these books are entirely made by actual humans and because of that, each choice is made based on social and cultural norms of the people involved. But the technical elements are fairly fixed because picture books are physical, tactile objects with some restrictions.

You'll notice that the paper used for very colorful books such as *Drawn Together* and *Love in the Library* is heavy and slick—almost like thick magazine paper. That is so the page can absorb the kinds of ink needed to achieve the detailed lines and colors without any kind of blur. If you look at books like *Fry Bread* where the illustrator uses more of a watercolor style of illustration, you'll see the pages are less slick but still heavy. These kinds of texture changes are noticeable to readers.

The use of white space is also an important element of a picture book's illustrations and design. Some illustrators use loads of action—lines, colors, images all over, including colored

The use of white space is also an important element of a picture book's illustrations and design.

backgrounds so that when and if they have an image sitting in a field of white, it means there is something important to attend to within that page. The white space can signal a change, a realization, or sometimes an important detail. On the other hand, some illustrators are more sparing within the images and colors used throughout a book. In this case, the white space is more distributed and might not be as noticeable. They may use other tools—such as changing to a colored background page—to signify a change in tone, mood, or action.

One other significant page design element is what is called a "bleed". This word refers to a lack of visible margins, where the reader can imagine that the image bleeds outside the confines of the page and into the universe. If you have a copy of *Fry Bread* handy, take a look at pages 10 and 11 and you'll see the choices that illustrator Juana Martinez-Neal made. First off, we see a big color shift from the more muted, golden-creamy sort of page color to a more vibrant and alive swirling blue, filled with stars and the sun. This visual shift complements a shift in perspective—from the more intimate images of people, hands, and stoves during the fry bread cooking process to an expansive universe that quite literally cannot be contained within the limits of the page.

PAGE TURNS

As adult readers, it's easy for us to forget the importance of page turns. In a novel the page turns are often simply a signal that the page ended and that the content of the book continues on the next page. But think about the blank space at the end of a chapter, or that extra space in the middle of a chapter. What does that extra space signal? The end of a scene? A change in point of view, or a change in the location of the action? This blank space, even in a novel, is a cue to the reader that something is changing.

In picture books the page turn is an even more important and purposeful design element. It controls the pacing of the book and is the one place where the reader holds all the power of the story in their (literal) hand. The reader can end it, or they can progress. They can retreat and revisit, or they can move forward. The author may have an idea or a desire for the way the book will be read, but the reader is in the driver's seat for this part of the experience. I always think it must be nerve wracking for picture book creators to decide where the page turn is going to happen, where the written text is going to leave off and pick up, and what kind of visual elements are going to stay and which are going to change across the pages.

In general, page turns in picture books are used to explore characters' actions and deepen the plot. But page turns can also be used to signal a change in place or time, introduce a new element to the story, change the point of view, or pose/answer a question (Sipe and Brightman 2009).

In general, page turns in picture books are used to explore characters' actions and deepen the plot.

Grab a picture book you've read before, and without reading the text, flip to any page and pause for a moment. What kind of scene is on the page? Is it a full page, a split page? Or does the illustration span both pages? Are the characters looking at you? At each other? Or are they more interested in the scenery? How do these pages make you feel? Relaxed? Curious?

Now, turn the page. Is the next page a place where more of the story is revealed? Is the new page deepening the story, adding complexity, and helping you understand what is at stake more clearly? Or perhaps there is a change in time and place? Or, best of all, a surprising turn, or explanation for a question you have been holding onto? That's the provocative power of page turns, the readerly act of making meaning is most active in these gaps—these reader-controlled pauses—where you, the readers, are in direct conversation with the text.

So, next time you are reading a picture book, take time to notice what is happening in the page turns, and allow students to explore the process as well.

ENDPAPERS (ALSO KNOWN AS END PAGES OR END SHEETS)

Picture book authors and illustrators have come to recognize the power of the "extra" real estate that exists in the endpapers of a book. Endpapers are another anatomic piece of the picture book that has evolved as technology has changed. The endpapers are exactly what they sound like; they are the paper that covers the inside of the covers and allows the book pages to be bound to the cover. In hardback picture books, endpapers are glued to the inside front and back covers. In paperback picture books, the end pages are sometimes printed on the insides of the covers.

Traditionally, picture book endpapers were pretty plain. Sometimes they might be a different color from the book, but often they were simply a heavier stock in the same color as the pages of the book.

But now, thanks to technology, endpapers can be used to help build suspense, provide important information, or for illustrators to have fun with the readers. For instance, in *Fry Bread*, the endpapers are used to extend the world of the book further than the limits of the story by listing Indigenous nations and communities (including some that are not federally recognized). Can you imagine the absolute honor and delight a reader would experience by finding their tribe listed on the endpapers among hundreds of others? The reality of seeing yourself and your community alongside so many others shows the fact that Indigenous folks are part of the here and now. The sovereign nations, tribes, and bands all share the space on the page, showing a powerful, political statement made on the end pages of a picture book.

AUTHORS' NOTES

I have a confession. I am dyslexic (why is it spelled like that?) and so reading, especially reading out loud, is a constant challenge for me. Because reading is difficult, I tend to want to GET TO THE STORY!!! And therefore, I have to make an effort to read the peritext—introductions, prefaces, forewords, endnotes, and authors' notes—all the stuff authors and publishers create in order to help me, the reader, make sense of the story. As a reader, however, I often just want to get into the story and block out everything else; I know that about myself and so instead of fighting it I incorporate this knowledge into my reading life. I read through a book once, without the peritext, and then I go back and often start the second read with the authors' notes or other peritext.

I have come to appreciate authors' notes because of Roland Barthes (1977). Remember him from Chapter 2? He's the guy who said the author was dead to the text as soon as the pen left the paper. Well, the author's note is a bit like a message in a bottle from that author.

The author's note is a bit like a message in a bottle from that author.

It is a way to provide much-needed context for the story, explanations of the time period or region, and important details, as well as providing a jumping off point for further study.

One of the best author's notes I have read is in Maggie Tokuda-Hall's *Love in the Library*. The book is a story of a sweet young couple, books, and finding happiness in times of government-enforced trauma. The characters, Tama and George, meet in the library of the Minidoka incarceration camp in Idaho during World War II. In her author's note, Tokuda-Hall provides us with a developmentally appropriate introduction to a piece of history that has been actively hidden and misrepresented. She writes:

> As much as I would hope this would be a story of a distant past, it is not. It's very much the story of America here and now. The racism that put my grandparents into Minidoka is the same hate that keeps children in cages on our border.
>
> *(Tokuda-Hall 2022)*

Tokuda-Hall's candor in the face of years of our country minimizing and omitting the effects of Order 9066 gives teachers and families a place to begin the kinds of history lessons we need. This straightforward naming is perhaps the most disruptive act possible in the face of the brutality of incarcerating people for existing, as well as the ongoing defense and erasure of this history. Tokuda-Hall's author's note ends "Because if we can fall in love, if we can find our joy, if we can find that miracle despite all of these truths—What else can we do?" (2022). Picture book authors like Tokuda-Hall are brilliant at presenting truth with hope, a skill both children and adult readers alike can learn from.

Of course, there are more features of a picture book's anatomy that you can explore. The spine, the gutter, the front and back flaps, the dedication page, even the copyright page (note: while a copyright page might seem boring, it often tells you how the illustrations were created which is a fascinating tidbit to share with children) are all important parts of this amazing creation we call picture books.

CHAPTER 3

CRITICAL VISUAL LITERACY IN CHILDREN'S LITERATURE

From time to time I realize how weird it is to be an adult who reads, thinks, teaches, and talks (somewhat incessantly) about children's books. But, I'm guessing if you are reading this, you are along for the ride, and you share my interest and concern about the ways children's experiences with literature have long-lasting effects. And you likely care deeply about children's reading lives. And with reason—there are tons of studies showing that getting kids to read is the absolute best way to get them to read more (and better!) (Stanovich 2009; Duke, Ward, and Pearson 2021). In fact, there is some evidence that providing materials that encourage children to read for pleasure might be the most effective reading intervention there is (Sun et al. 2024).

And one of the easiest ways to get kids to read is to value what *they* want to read, to engage them with interesting, compelling, and complex stories that allow them to explore the world with literature. This is a hard ask for many adults who imagine that "protecting the children" means isolating students from complex ideas and histories. Some of the complexities of life—such as liking someone who doesn't like you back; parents getting divorced; not fitting in; making mistakes; and wrestling with the unfairness of the power and privilege—can all be found inside great children's literature.

> Adults tend to think that kids don't recognize or wrestle with issues of power and privilege, but they do, every day.

Adults tend to think that kids don't recognize or wrestle with issues of power and privilege, but they do, every day. Kids bear witness to and experience first-hand racism, sexism, homophobia, ableism, and all the other ills that our society inflicts on itself. They see the actions of individuals and the ways systems are designed, and when kids start to call out or struggle with these patently unfair issues, adults often panic in recognition because the reflection we see isn't pretty. When our traumas are shown to us in bright neon letters, it often leads to comments like "be nice", "be kind", "don't say/do/ask about that", or the more direct, "nice people don't talk about ... sex, politics, race, difference, money, etc." with no actual explanation. Adults can be incredibly invested in protecting an uncontested vantage point of privilege rather than investing in changing systems that maintain a toxic status quo. After all, we, as a society, are marinating in oppressive views of the world that uphold a warped view of "normal" so that anyone who exists outside that idealized norm (white, straight, cis, male, Christian, abled, middle class) is unprotected, unsupported, and actively marginalized. If we admit that unfair treatment exists, we also have to admit the shame of being an active and willing participant in an unfair and inhumane world.

I wonder sometimes how adults can be both overly anxious about and completely disinterested in the content of children's literature. I get that we all contain multitudes and this is just one example of the joyous discontinuity of adulthood, but for folks to *not* read and then also dismiss books written for children is mind boggling.

In this chapter we are going to look more carefully at the intricate ways that images, especially, carry social norms, stereotypes, and messages about who is valued and deserving and who is othered and less than.

SOME DEFINITIONS AND CLARIFICATIONS

Words matter and having a common understanding of what we mean when we use various terms makes it easier to learn new ideas and concepts. What is important to know is that I am not saying these are the *only* definitions of these words and ideas. Rather, these are the definitions we are going to use together.

Critical visual literacy. Let's break down this term because there is a lot of action happening in this three-word phrase.

Critical in this case does not refer to "critical thinking" or blaming or heaping criticism on someone. We are not going to be assigning "0 out of 5 stars". Instead, I am using critical and criticality in the ways that law professors like Derrick Bell, Kimberlé Crenshaw, Richard Delgado, Cheryl Harris wrote about back in the 1970s. Critical Race Theory is a lens we can use to focus on and critique the ways power and privilege are at work in our society. It is *not* a way to blame or inflict guilt on individuals. For a deeper understanding, I recommend reading *Critical Race Theory: The Key Writings That Formed the Movement* (Crenshaw et al. 1995); *Critical Race Theory: An Introduction* (Delgado and Stefancic 2023); and "Where Are We? Critical Race Theory in Education 20 Years Later" (Dixson and Rousseau Anderson 2018)

Visual. Ok, that's pretty much what you think it is. Visual as in "seen" or "shown". Think about all the parts of a book that convey meaning through shape, color, and other design elements including fonts, page layouts, and images. It is all the things that go into literature that rely on the reader's visual interpretation

Literacy ... yup. Reading. But, in this case, I am talking about making meaning, not simply decoding. Think about the tone, voice, point of view, and vocabulary that all have to be read and understood to get the meaning of the text

Put it all together and you have critical visual literacy, a field of study specific to picture books and graphic novels that asks how readers make sense of the visual elements that hold social, cultural, and emotional cues.

The reason for bringing a critical visual literacy lens to children's literature is to bring to the surface the ways our systems—specifically our educational systems—communicate, re-emphasize, and entrench racist, ableist, homophobic ideals in our children. And, maybe more importantly, critical visual literacy also gives us a tool for choosing amazing books to share with children.

CRITICAL LITERACY: READING WITH POWER AND PRIVILEGE IN MIND

The idea of power and privilege in children's literature starts early. Recall the story of *The Rainbow Fish* which we briefly discussed on page 15. This picture book is the cornerstone of many preschool and kindergarten lessons that focus on friendship and empathy. If you don't remember the plot, here is a brief and biased summary.

The Rainbow Fish enjoys the way his scales shine and throw rainbows. He's not particularly outgoing or interested in the other fish on the reef but he's also not a jackass. One day a fish comes to him and asks for one of his rainbow scales. Rainbow Fish says no, and so, naturally, the entire reef turns their fins up in disgust and freezes him out. They ostracize him because he won't give his scales away. He feels a certain way about all this and talks to a starfish who recommends the wise octopus to answer the question of what to do about the fact that Rainbow Fish has no friends. The octopus tells him to "Give a glittering scale to each of the other fish" and so he does and everyone lives happily ever after.

Think about the message this story is sending. If you've ever met a fish in real life, what happens when you rip the scales off? I mean, if you are not trying to kill it, descaling is not a good idea, they need those scales! Scales protect fish from the elements and scales are—LITERALLY—attached to them. So in order to avoid being ostracized or to fit in and be accepted, the solution, according to *The Rainbow Fish*, is to rip part of yourself off and hand it to somebody else who desires it.

Additionally, note the petty jealousy about the fact that Rainbow Fish has these cool scales—scales that are different than the norm—that have to be stripped away and distributed. Differences have to be tempered and flattened in order to preserve sameness. Let's be clear, if I'm walking down the street, and you holler over at me—"Hey! I like that shirt". Am I supposed to rip it off and throw it at you? Because I'm not doing that.

This process of considering a piece of literature through the lens of power and privilege is called critical literacy. We often

This process of considering a piece of literature through the lens of power and privilege is called critical literacy.

ask young readers to consider the "author's message" as they read a text. However, it is perhaps even more important to go a step further and ask: *What do I, as the reader, think about the author's message? Do I agree? Do I disagree? What implications does the author's message have beyond the book?* This is critical literacy.

Now, let's dig into the ways *images* can reinforce unquestioned stereotypes, and how we can use critical *visual* literacy to consider these issues.

HOW IMAGES CAN REINFORCE (OR DISRUPT) STEREOTYPES AND TROPES

The best way to recognize the ways literature presents differences from the idealized norm (white, straight, abled, cis, middle class, Christian) as inherently problematic is to carefully examine images that communicate messages (especially stereotypes and tropes) to young readers. For my work, I think of stereotypes as overgeneralizations based on scant evidence that successfully place people as *other*. This literal *othering* helps us separate ourselves from groups of people that society sees as less valuable. *Stereotypes*, biased assumptions about groups of people, carry an enormous amount of power because they are the stories that are told about us, to us. And, worst of all, sometimes they are believed by us.

Tropes are images and figures of speech—often metaphorical—that are shortcuts for larger ideas. Imagine a western movie where a man walks into a bar wearing a black cowboy hat. What does seeing that black hat perched on his head communicate about him as a character? His place in the story? What can we expect from him? There are lots of subtle and not so subtle images and phrases used in books that carry meaning.

I'll be walking you through the critical visual literacy process of noticing and naming using Sophie Blackall's picture book, *If You Come to Earth* (2020). The publisher describes the picture book as "a glorious guide to our home planet, and a call for us to take care of both Earth and each other". In the book there is a double-page spread that illustrates all the different kinds of families there are here on earth.

First, look over the entire illustration (Figure 3.1). What catches your eye? Maybe the red blanket up in the right-hand corner? Maybe the large

FIGURE 3.1
An illustration from *If You Come to Earth*

white polka-dotted blanket in the middle? Perhaps the motion line of the bouncing ball going down the middle of the page? And what about those folks on the bike (the only people not on the green grass)? Sometimes there are questions without answers, sometimes the questions aren't that important, but they are still questions and the process of noticing is important. Book design and color theory give us some indications of what might be attended to first as we view the illustration from *If You Come to Earth*. But that doesn't help us read critically—so instead, I am going to walk you through using both visual and critical literacy to surface some ideas that are there, but may be hidden if you don't use both these lenses.

PROCESS FOR ENGAGING IN CRITICAL VISUAL LITERACY

Here is the general process we'll use for engaging in critical visual literacy:

- **Step 1: Chunk apart the page.** While taking a look at the whole page first is important, analyzing the entire page at once can be overwhelming. By taking chunks of a larger image you are better able to focus and discern meaning
- **Step 2: Name who you see.** Use direct language to name race, gender, sexual orientation, ability, socio-economic status, and religious affiliation
- **Step 3: Notice details.** Part of the exercise is to surface and challenge what we see and to admit how we interpret images
- **Step 4: Think about the stereotypes we tell (related to what you have named in Step 2).** Recognize what society asserts as "normal" or "natural"—especially the ugly underbelly of white, patriarchal, Christian supremacy that we are enmeshed within every day of our existence in this country
- **Step 5: Ask: How are the images aligned with or in opposition to these stereotypes?** Compare the image to the stereotypes and "othering" messages
- **Step 6:** If, after engaging this process, we conclude that this isn't a book we want to share with children in our classrooms, **what's another book (focus on #OwnVoices) we might read instead?**

Now let's practice taking a critical visual literacy lens on each part of the two-page spread from *If You Come to Earth* by Sophie Blackall. While we'll be looking at small parts of the whole illustration, you may want to also flip back to view the full image in Figure 3.1.

Being Black at the Park

Step 1: Chunk apart the page

Since in English we read left to right and top to bottom, a reader might first notice the Black family on the blue blanket in the upper left corner of the page. Let's zoom in on that part of the spread (Figure 3.2) and talk through the stereotypes and tropes that are being asserted.

FIGURE 3.2
A Black family in the park in *If You Come to Earth* (full illustration in Figure 3.1)

Step 2: Name who you see.

- A Black mother, pregnant with four kids of various ages from very young to a teen

Step 3: Notice details.

- Five half-sandwiches, no other food or drink
- A checkers board
- A wild-eyed little black and white dog with alert ears pulling on a leash

Step 4: Think about the stereotypes we tell about Black families.

- Absent fathers, multiple fathers, lots of children
- Economic insecurity/food insecurity
- Unruly and loud, lack of parental control or rule following

Step 5: How are the images aligned with or in opposition to stereotypes about Black families?
There is no co-parent in the image of the Black family and they are not expecting one to arrive (see the five half-sandwiches). The kids are close in age and the mother is pregnant again. She is also not paying much attention to the kids. Instead, she is sort of staring off into the middle distance—thus reifying the idea that Black parents are somewhat disconnected from their children. The dog is pulling at the leash and looks a bit wild eyed—which signals that it is not well-trained.

What else do you notice and think about in this image?

Step 6: What's another book that centers Black families that we might read instead?

- *It's Pride, Baby!* (2024) written by Allen R. Wells, illustrated by Dia Valle
- *Octopus Stew* (2021) by Eric Velasquez
- *Marley and the Family Band* (2022) written by Cedella Marley and Tracey Baptiste, illustrated by Tiffany Rose

Islamic Femininity

Step 1: Chunk apart the page.

As we continue to study the full illustration (Figure 3.1), we might begin to focus on the image of the Muslim mother and child on their orange and white blanket (Figure 3.3).

Step 2: Name who you see.

- A woman in a hijab sits face to face with her daughter, sharing tea

Step 3: Notice details.

They are sitting very close to one another on a small blanket. There is no indication that they are even aware of others in the park or interested in activities going on close at hand.

FIGURE 3.3
A Muslim mother and daughter in the park in *If You Come to Earth* (full illustration in Figure 3.1)

Step 4: Think about the stereotypes we tell about Muslim families and women.

Many stereotypes around Muslim families are based on the idea that men are missing from family life and that the women are shy, isolated, or repressed.

Step 5: How are the images aligned with or in opposition to stereotypes about Muslim families and women?

This image reinforces the idea that men are not present in family life as there is no room for another parent or partner on the blanket to share the moment of peace. Once again, we have a non-white mother without a partner. In addition, there is an isolation or self-segregation to these two. They don't see, recognize, or show any interest in anyone else in the park.

What do you notice here? What have I missed?

Step 6: What's another book that centers Muslim families that we might read instead?

- *Insha'Allah, No, Maybe So* (2024) written by Rhonda Roumani and Nadia Roumani, illustrated by Olivia Aserr
- *The Proudest Blue: A Story of Hijab and Family* (2019) written by Ibtihaj Muhammad, illustrated by S.K. Ali Hatem Aly
- *Amira's Picture Day* (2021) written by Reem Faruqi, illustrated by Fahmida Azim

Gay Dads

Step 1: Chunk apart the page.

Below the Muslim family and closer to the reader, we see another, larger picnic blanket and a family with two gay dads (Figure 3.4).

Step 2: Name who you see.

- Two men with one toddler, sitting on a large, striped, blanket. The blanket is comparable in size to that of the other families in the illustration

FIGURE 3.4
Gay dads and their baby in the park in *If You Come to Earth* (full illustration in Figure 3.1)

Step 3: Notice details.

- On the blanket there are three dishes, a cake box, a cake, as well as what appears to be a diaper bag
- One man sits with the cake in front of him, gazing at the toddler. The other dad kneels and feeds the toddler
- The cake is pink and the child's onesie is green

Step 4: Think about the stereotypes we tell about gay parents.
Gay parents are stereotyped as white, cis, male, overeducated, living in swanky urban or suburban places with loads of money. These men are often

portrayed as prim, proper, sassy, flamboyant, and absolutely committed to using their child as the ultimate adornment. These portrayals subvert their identity as gay men to become neutered and sexless parents that exist somewhere between the idealized and binary heterosexual roles of straight couples. They are allowed to be affectionate to the children, but they are no longer able to show affection to each other lest they make their straight counterparts uncomfortable.

Step 5: How are the images aligned with or in opposition to stereotypes about gay parents?

The gay men depicted on this page are both wholly invested in the child and absolutely uninterested in and separated from each other. In fact, they are further apart from one another than any other adults in the illustration, leaving one parent isolated from his family. The relative affluence of the couple is reflected in the size of the blanket compared to the number of people. In other words, the blanket is similar in size to that of other families but since there is only one child there are more resources. In fact, the cake is huge for three people!

Keep going—what are you seeing?

Step 6: What's another book that centers LGBTQIA+ families that we might read instead?

- *Bathe the Cat* (2022) written by Alice B. McGinty, illustrated by David Roberts
- *Grandad's Camper* (2021) by Harry Woodgate
- *My Footprints* (2019) written by Bao Phi, illustrated by Basia Tran

Your Turn!

Let's move now to the right side of the illustration (Figure 3.1). Take a look at the family shown in Figure 3.5. First, identify what you see, then think about what that might mean. Make sure to think about the family as a whole and the individuals within the family. What do you notice about gender? Marital status? Sexual orientation? Culture? What do you notice specifically about the kids? What are the boys doing?

FIGURE 3.5
A Jewish family in the park in *If You Come to Earth* (full illustration in Figure 3.1)

What are the girls doing? What kinds of gender roles are enforced or challenged and why? Remember, you do not have to believe the stereotype, and you don't have to share what you write with anyone else. But, you have to be honest because images communicate messages and those messages matter. All of the observations are just that—they are assumptions, based on very little evidence. There is no right or wrong. Work through the critical visual literacy in Table 5 as completely and honestly as you can.

TABLE 5

YOU TRY IT!: USING CRITICAL VISUAL LITERACY TO NOTICE AND NAME
Step 1: Chunk apart the page.
Step 2: Name who you see. Use direct language to name race, gender, sexual orientation, ability, socio-economic status, and religious affiliation.
Step 3: Notice details. Part of the exercise is to surface and challenge what we see and how we interpret that image.
Step 4: Think about the stereotypes we tell (related to what you have named in Step 2).
Step 5: Ask: How are the images aligned with or in opposition to these stereotypes? Compare the image to the stereotypes and “othering” messages.
Step 6: If, after engaging this process, we conclude that this isn’t a book we want to share with children in our classrooms, **what’s another book (focus on #OwnVoices) we might read instead?**

HOW DO WE START? BREAKING DOWN IMAGES TO GAIN CRITICAL MEANING

Books, especially image-rich picture books, graphic novels, and comics, have the opportunity to expand children's views of the world, people, history, and society. Images don't just hang out on books like neutral hotel paintings. At their best, images and words provide opportunities for readers to think, see, and learn. The ways images, colors, fonts, page turns, and words work together to enhance, expand, contradict, clarify, and complexify a story create the full reading experience.

At their best, images and words provide opportunities for readers to think, see, and learn.

Images carry enormous social meaning, especially for emergent readers who are wrestling with decoding, vocabulary, grammar, punctuation, and sequence. These readers may rely on images to make meaning of the text when their decoding is stressed. Books use images to clue in readers to everything from changes in mood, point of view, time and place. Images can be used to provide important and additional information that changes the story. Most importantly, books that utilize both images and text provide readers with the possibility to deeply engage and discover new worlds, to critically interpret the worlds they see, and give rise to important questions.

And we, as adult gatekeepers, have to wrestle with the fact that books also provide an arena to simply enforce toxic, unrecognized biases, to reiterate traumatic beliefs, and to erase entire people and experiences.

Now that you have a framework and a process for critical visual literacy, go and look at some of your favorite books. Who is represented? How are stereotypes preserved and promoted? Or, better still, do you see stereotypes being disrupted? In what ways can you talk about these ideas and raise those issues with your students?

To support yourself and others in this process, I've included the Critical Visual Literacy Worksheet in Appendix B. You can use this worksheet with the students in your classes, or with colleagues, as a way to make concrete the ideas and notions that too often go unrecognized and unchallenged.

DIDJA KNOW? FORMATS, FORMS, GENRES, AND WHY THEY MATTER

That's right! It's definitions time ... again. And, again, no shame or shade if any of these terms are new to you. We are just here for clarification. Formats, forms, and genres are all important concepts in children's literature. And, it's important for teachers not to simply understand these ideas, but also understand the kinds of affordances literature can provide readers. But, why should teachers care? Simply put, when you find books that kids will read, you open the door to them becoming invested, avid readers.

FORMAT

On the most basic level, the form of a book is how we talk about the ways books, as objects, exist and tell the story. This is the most concrete aspect of a book. Is it a picture book? A novel? A graphic novel? Or a novel in verse? Each of these forms have some generalized rules and, of course, instances when authors break those rules. Additionally, any story can be told in any format! The format is not the constraining factor. Read on and you'll get the hang of it.

Picture book. (We've talked about picture books a lot already in this book, but here it is again for easy reference!) Often thirty-two pages, often hard cover. Often oriented for the pages to be wider than they are tall (10 inches by 7 or 8 inches). This wide orientation allows for a larger image field, especially for double-page spreads. Most of the page is filled with images with less space used for written text. The design elements are an important aspect of the storytelling.

Novel. Can be any page length, separated into chapters, predominantly written text. Hard or soft cover. What can I say ... these are the generic idea of a book. Any genre, any form, written for a multitude of audiences.

Graphic novel. Related to but not exactly the same as comic books. Can be any page length and, much like picture books, use images and written text to create something unique. There are specific design elements such as font, color, panels, speech bubbles, and captions that you also might see in other illustrated books like the *Diary of a Wimpy Kid* novels by Jeff Kinney, or in picture books like Shaun Tan's *The Arrival* (2007).

Graphic novels produced for Western audiences are read from left to right and top to bottom. Panels contain the "scenes" that convey the information about the genre, the characters, the plot, and the setting. All of that information must be gleaned by the reader from both the images, the (minimal, compared to a novel) text, and the sequence in which all the information is given. And then there is the gutter—the spaces between panels. This is where the reader really shines! They set the pace and do the hard work of putting the pieces of the multimodal of the reading experience together. The gutters, much like the page turns in picture books, are where the reader is in control and where the important sense making happens—the reader might slow down or speed up depending on their understanding of the story. They might realize something isn't making sense and trace their way back through the book to reread and reevaluate either the text or the illustrations. For instance, the reader might notice a color change from one panel to another and want to pause to think about the importance of that change; they might begin to notice a recurrent image and wonder if it means something; or, they might predict what action is coming. All of these elements combine to make graphic novels a recursive and complex sense making reading process.

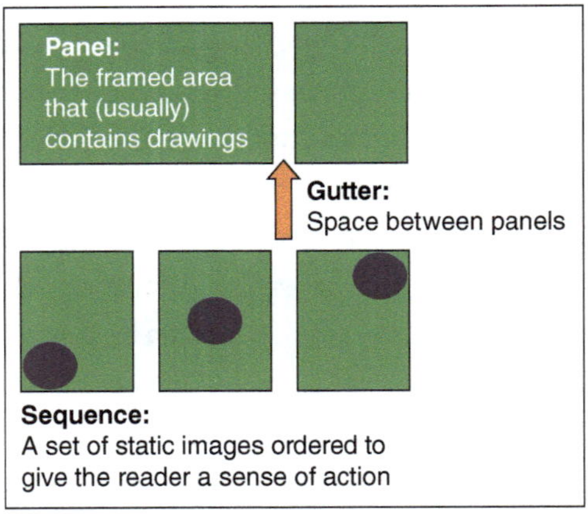

FIGURE DK.2

Panels and gutters are elements of graphic novels that contribute to the reader's sense making of the text as a whole.

Like all the other media formats, graphic novels can and do come in different sizes, genres, and forms.

FORMS

Speaking of forms (different from formats!), let's get into them. Forms are a little squishier than formats, but there are still fairly agreed upon guidelines. Again, you can present any kind of story with any form. Think of it as the writing style more than anything.

Prose. This is the sort of regular, everyday composition style. It's, you know, regular language used in regular ways where nothing about the meaning of the text is really riding on design elements like line breaks, page breaks, or fonts. Most literature, fiction, and non-fiction is written in prose form. Look at picture books like *Separate is Never Equal* (2014) by Duncan Tonatiuh, or a novel like *The Marrow Thieves* (2017) by Cherie Dimaline, and you'll find prose.

Epistolary. This category falls under the prose form but its definition is just a little more dependent on constraints. Epistolary novels are novels written in letter or diary form. These include dystopian fiction such as *Parable of the Sower* (2019) by Octavia Butler, coming of age and coming out LGBTQIA+ YA novels like *Dear Rachel Maddow* (2019) by Adrienne Kisner, and middle grade novels about racism and anti-Black police violence such as *Dear Martin* (2018) by Nic Stone. This form provides the reader with a real look at what is happening within the internal life of the narrator.

Poetry. A special word on poetry. Poetry is a way of playing with and using written and oral language by attending to the rhythm (sometimes), rhyme schemes (sometimes), as well as the literal arrangement of written text on the page (almost always). And poetry is often used in picture books as well as novels in verse. Poetry can also be used in combination with other forms such as *Dear Mothman* (2023) by Robin Gow which is both an epistolary novel and a novel in verse featuring a trans boy finding a way forward after his best friend dies.

Wordless. Lastly, a word on *wordless* literature. There are wordless (or almost wordless) picture books like *Home in a Lunchbox* (2024) by Cherry Mo, in which Jun, newly arrived from Hong Kong, shows us what it feels like to be in a new school trying to figure out every single thing in a new language and a new culture. Wordless books communicate complex emotional narratives solely with images. There are also wordless books like *The Only Child* (2015) by Guojing which bends the reader's expectations by starting off as if it were a simple story of a small child trying to make their way to their grandmother's house and turning into a magical journey in the clouds with the help of a very understanding elk.

Formats and forms are important for teachers to think about because some of our students will be particularly drawn to some formats such as graphic novels or specific forms, like poetry. Unfortunately, literary gatekeepers—teachers, parents, curriculum designers—often act as if there is some sort of hierarchy to literary formats or forms. There is a huge and terrible cost that students pay for the literary gatekeeping of adults based on their own nostalgia, preference, or unfounded belief. These biases flow directly from these adults' own experiences and preferences and have tremendous impact on what is deemed acceptable in the classroom. Research consistently finds that neither the form nor the format is an important factor when determining which books help grow students' reading motivation and comprehension (Allington 1977). Instead, providing a wide array of text topics and types of literature only helps provide readers with places to grow into the readers they can be.

The most important thing to remember—if you want kids to read, then Let. Them. Read.

GENRE

Here is the part I've been avoiding. There is no other literary element that will devolve into spilled lattes, pulled ascots, and pointedly caustic and completely obscure insults than an argument about genres with a group of PhDs.

At their root, genres are simply a way to categorize stories. If you go into a bookstore, you might see books categorized by topics like Cooking; Self help; Reference; Kids' Books. If you sign on to a streaming service, you might see Rom-Com; Action; LGBTQIA+; Horror; Documentary and so on. These categories are all equally useful, but I want to take a step back and examine why we want to put these kinds of borders around stories.

Categorizations help us put things into buckets of expectations that some folks agree on, but those buckets can (and do) change across time, place, need, tradition, and culture. Defining genres is like trying to determine a toddler's shoe size by chasing them around Disneyland. There is so much movement, excitement, fear, and joy that the point of the event is sometimes lost on the need to impose structure. Genres help us understand some general expectations and yet genres are permeable in very unexpected ways.

Genres help us understand some general expectations and yet genres are permeable in very unexpected ways.

In general, I subscribe to a fairly simple map of genres and genre expectations that includes Realistic Fiction; Historical Fiction; Fantasy; Biography and Memoir. The reason for these particular categorizations is that they help us understand how literary elements such as *setting, plot,* and *character* interact and affect reading expectations. Think about these elements and the ways different genres rely on each element.

Setting—The time and place of the story
Plot—The actions that happen to the characters within the story
Character—The person (or thing) that the actions are happening to

Within each genre different literary elements (setting, plot, and character) take up more or less importance. Readers sometimes connect with these literary elements in different ways. For instance, some readers love rich, sensual stories filled with smells, tactile elements, and detailed times and places. Stories set in deep gullies, with horses galloping in squelchy moss smelling mud on moonlit nights filled with the smell of wild roses (or some such nonsense) might capture some readers. While others care more about the ways the characters connect, feel, express themselves endlessly about their emotions, desires, observations, memories, and hopes for the future and other ridiculousness. While others—some might label these readers "correct"—really just want things to freakin' happen in a story because why else are we here but to find out what the freak happened and why?!?!?

So, when thinking about the books you might bring into the class, or share with students, or leave laying around to entice them like a shy

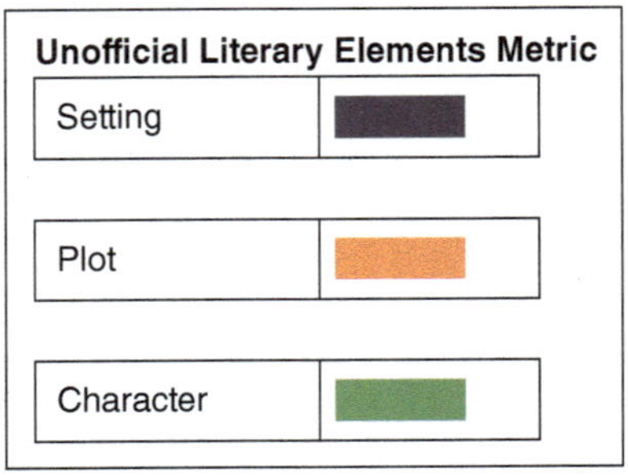

FIGURE DK.3
Literary elements such as setting, plot and character are (generally) weighted differently in different genres of text.

water buffalo to the watering hole, think about what kinds of stories your students might want. I like to use a handy dandy, totally unscientific metric that looks something like Figure DK.3 to show the weight of different literary elements that a particular genre relies on—in general.

Realistic Fiction

Stories in this genre occur in the here and now, in real places that adhere to the physical rules of reality. We have already read about some examples of realistic fiction including *Dear Martin* or *Home in a Lunchbox*. These books are contemporary to the time in which they are written. That's the part that can be a little tricky. The books stay in that time, but the world keeps moving. Other examples of realistic fiction are books such as *The Outsiders* (1967) and *The Great Gatsby* (1925) which are novels of their times—with all the racism, classism, misogyny, and homophobia that was all too prevalent. Just because time moves forward and technology, science, and our understanding of human rights moves forward does not make these books historical. The story is contemporary to the time in which they were written.

In general, realistic fiction is more concerned with the WHAT and the WHO over the where and the when. So, if you were going to show the weight of the literary elements, it might look something like Figure DK.4.

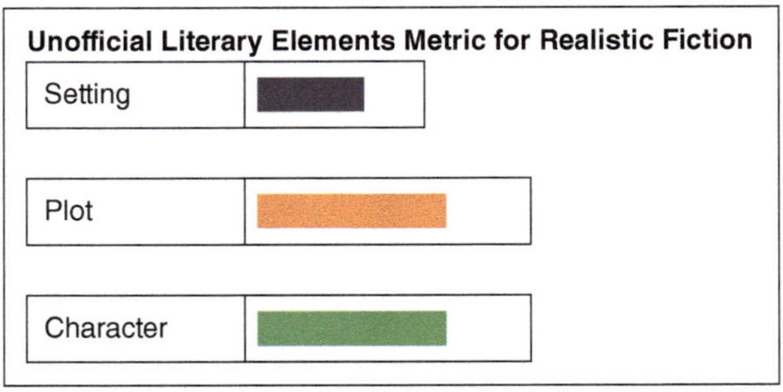

FIGURE DK.4
Plot and characters typically drive the story in realistic fiction.

Historical Fiction

Books in this genre are set in the long (or not so long) ago and are based on real events or times. Duncan Tonatiuh's picture book, *Separate is Never Equal,* is set in the 1940s and tells the story of Sylvia Mendez, her family, and the little known landmark lawsuit around school desegregation in California prior to Brown v. Board of Education. If you want more romance in your historical fiction, read Melinda Lo's award-winning YA novel *Last Night at the Telegraph Club* (2021) set in San Francisco in the 1950s which tells a gorgeous story of two young women (one white and one Chinese) falling in love before Stonewall, before LGBTQIA+ marriage, before they had the right to exist. And, I hate to break it to you, there are a bunch of books set in the 1970s and 80s that are historical fiction. Look into Eric Gansworth's *If I Ever Get Out of Here* (2013) and *Give Me Some Truth* (2018) about a Native American teen dealing with ... well, everything in the very familiar (to some of us) decades of our own childhood with a fabulous musical track of the times.

Again, generally speaking, historical fiction is more dependent on characters and setting, and less about plot (Figure DK.5)

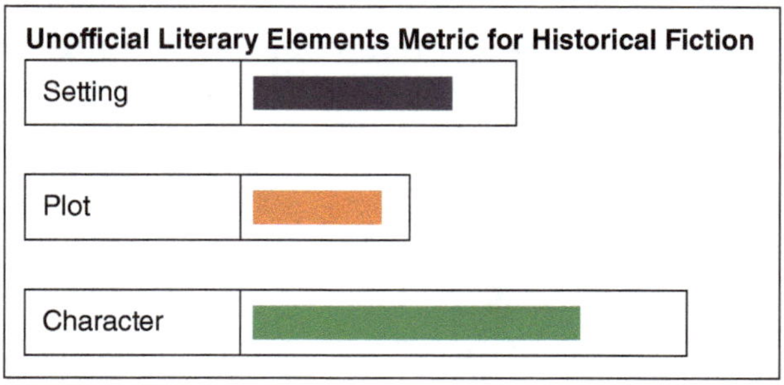

FIGURE DK.5

Setting and characters are often the stronger literary elements in historical fiction.

Fantasy

This genre offers us a huge and diverse bucket of books. I think of fantasy as narratives in which the known laws of our universe are suspended. This suspension can be because of technology or magic, but either way there is no telling what is going to happen when you walk through a door, or drop a pen, or start your first day at a new school. I know I am going to get a lot of static about this, but magic and science are the same in these

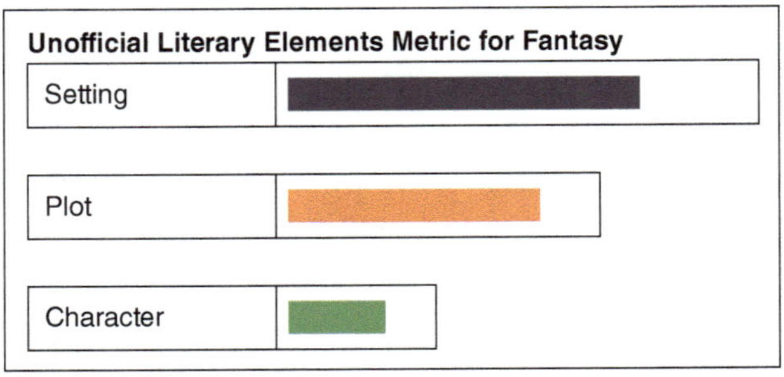

FIGURE DK.6
Setting rules in the genre of fantasy.

stories. They both represent something happening that is impossible in our current world—be it hover cars or talking dragons, magic amulets or laser swords, it is all equally impossible in the here and now.

The element of fantasy that is incredibly important is what is often called "world building" which refers to the author's work of ... well, building out the world where the story is going to occur, also known as Setting. The reader has to believe that a great flood or war or other event changed the face of the world and left us with districts or factions or zones and that only a small group of teens can save us from crumbling away. Readers need to be able to drape the words around them and immerse themselves in this new reality where witches bake potions into sweets, or add other people's memory cores into their heads. No other genre is more dependent on scene setting than fantasy (Figure DK.6).

Biography and Memoir

Biographies and memoirs are narratives that are either about important people or important events. And while texts in this genre are nonfiction, in many cases the "truth" is a little stretchable. Biographies and memoirs reveal the truth as the author sees it. Biographies and memoirs are built on how the author chooses to represent both the person and the time. There can be many books written about a single person or event—each one from a different perspective or in a different format.

Biographies are often written by third parties that take an interest in either an event or a person or both. Take a look at children's books about Claudette Colvin, Cesar Chavez and Dolores Huerta, or Harvey Milk. Each time a story is written by a different biographer or in a different time, it provides a slightly different slice of the person's life or look at the event.

Memoirs are even more subjective than biographies—and that isn't a bad thing. Memoirs are first-person narratives, written by the person who experienced a time or event. Readers can fact-check the events referenced in a memoir but the form itself is more focused on how the person was affected or how they felt or what they thought about the events. Books like *Farewell to Manzanar* (1973) by Jeanne Wakatsuki Houston or *Brown Girl Dreaming* (2014) by Jacqueline Woodson are memoirs that provide windows into lives that are extraordinary and worthy of study in everyday classrooms.

For these stories, the time and place are important, but really, if we are not highly invested in the person on whom the memoir focuses, then there is no reason to turn the page (Figure DK.7). I need to feel a sense of outrage or admiration when the main character hits the page. I need to root for them, to feel personally attached to their actions as well as their feelings.

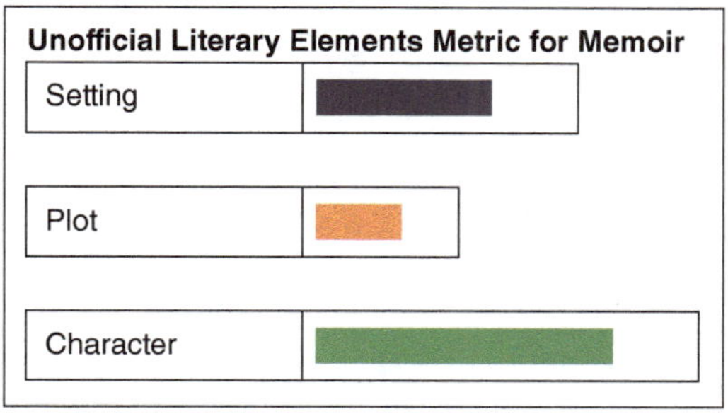

FIGURE DK.7
The main character is usually the most important element of a memoir.

LOOK, HERE'S THE DEAL

Now that we have some shared understanding of forms, formats, and genres and why they matter for readers, we can use these understandings to help curate a diverse collection of books for the classroom. We can choose books that entice and speak to different readers. We can make better recommendations. And perhaps, we can even understand ourselves better as readers.

We can choose books that entice and speak to different readers. We can make better recommendations. And perhaps, we can even understand ourselves better as readers.

Here are some questions that might help you to identify reader preferences, that go beyond "What's your favorite book?"

1. What's your favorite food? [This is just a warm-up question to get a conversation started, especially helpful for readers who don't see themselves as readers and have been proven right over and over again.]

2. What's your favorite video game? And why? [Genre info is hidden in this question. Do they like character games like Justice League? Fantasy like World of Warcraft? Or, strategy games like Age of Empire or Minecraft? If they like Minecraft, what is it they enjoy? The creation/destruction of solo play or the survival aspect?]

3. What's your favorite TV, movie, website, YouTube, TikTok channel? [This gets to the kind of voice and style they might enjoy. Do they like goofy stuff or serious drama? Are they going on the web to find information? Are they into fanfic of some kind?]

4. What book—specific book—did you hate and why? [This question is meant to communicate that it is perfectly fine to dislike a book. And it tells you why they had a hard time with it. Was it boring? Was it assigned? Was it too easy? Too much talking and emotion? All of these are important aspects to understand about this reader right in front of you.]

Each reader has the right to read something that captures their attention. They have the right to read something that interests, engages, and even upsets them. And, it is our responsibility, as the adults, to help young readers in classrooms find what it is that they love and to provide lots of options to explore. Readers have the right to change their minds, to explore forms, formats, and genres. They have the right to say "I loved this, but not that" without shame or shade.

And, perhaps most importantly, the adults in the room must give up our own ego about what is good or bad literature. Just because I love a genre or format doesn't mean it is the best. It simply means it holds an affinity for me.

CHAPTER 4

INSIDERS AND OUTSIDERS: WHO'S WRITING, WHO'S WATCHING, AND WHY IT MATTERS

Ok, how are you doing at this point? It's been a lot: genres, forms, narrative, tokenism, along with loads of information about systems, power, nostalgia, and privilege. I know it's later in the book. We have been through a lot. You are probably hoping for an easy chapter—something with cute animals and squishy-cheeked babies. But, no. Instead we are going to be looking at how to put all this together. Don't panic, you got this. Besides, this work is only happening in a book for now, so it is perfectly safe.

I want to introduce you to a legal scholar who has been incredibly influential to many folks in teacher education—including me. Kimberlé Crenshaw is one of a group of legal minds that brought us Critical Race Theory (see Chapter 3). Her legal work related to violence against women of color led her to create a way to name and understand the intersections of race and gender. Crenshaw uses the term intersectionality to explain the ways *multiple* marginalized identities are additive (1991). In other words, people with multiple marginalized identities (Black women, for example) are further marginalized by the legal system (and really all systems) in this country.

Crenshaw's argument is that the US legal system was created by, and is maintained to support, white, straight, middle class, Christian, cisgender, men without disabilities. The system is simply not capable of supporting anyone who does not conform to this idealized norm. And although Crenshaw used race and gender as a starting point for her work, she reminds us that this framework can be used across many identities. "For example, race can also be a coalition of straight and gay people of color, and thus serve as a basis for critique of churches and other cultural institutions that reproduce heterosexism" (Crenshaw 1991, 1299). The greater the degree of difference from the idealized norm, the more marginalized a person is. I recognize, as do other scholars, the same assumed normative standard at work in education (Tefera, Powers, and Fischman 2018; Ladson-Billings and Tate 2022). After all, oppression has a pretty thin playbook that gets shared across systems so let's work on recognizing, dismantling, and creating something better than the status quo.

The greater the degree of difference from the idealized norm, the more marginalized a person is.

As educators who select children's literature for the classroom, it is important that we pay attention to multiple aspects of representation. It's up to us to carefully select and amplify children's literature that allows for students to experience a myriad of marginalized representations by authors from those communities. I want to use the lens of intersectionality in this chapter and really explore how teachers can center intersectionality in the ELA work they do in the classroom.

When we start putting it all together, we need to keep several big ideas in mind—like those performers we see in tourist areas juggling a saw, a bowling ball, and a bowl of soup. You may be familiar with Bishop's metaphor of books as mirrors, windows, and sliding glass doors. Bishop wrote that readers can experience a book as a mirror that reflects their ways of being in the world, a window that they can see other ways of being in the world, or a sliding glass door in which the reader can visit a new way of being in the world (1990). I want to reiterate that this idea means that #OwnVoice literature is for everyone ... these books can be mirrors for some people, windows for others, and, if they are engaging and exciting books, they have the possibility of being sliding glass doors. Got that? Perfect.

Now let's add intersectionality to the mix. By utilizing the ideas from intersectionality in children's literature we have to examine books for *multi-faceted* representations—both for the representation simply existing and for the quality of that representation. We need to learn to notice, appreciate, and critically engage with the identities across race, ethnicity, language, gender, sexuality, ability, religion, and class, and so on. And look, I know this is hard. We love to pigeonhole people into tiny, unidimensional identities. If a student has an IEP, the document absolutely outweighs any other identity such as gender or race. Can a Latina actually be a lesbian and remain Latina? Oh! And, we love a good binary ... male or female; Black or white; straight or gay; disabled or nondisabled; and on and on. (Can you hear my sarcasm in these sentences?) Intersectionality recognizes that we all have multiple facets to our identities, and that marginalized identities are additive in the ways they remove us from the support of the idealized norm.

And, keep in mind, when I use the term "marginalized" I mean communities of people who are purposefully kept from power within our society. In other words, we are not talking about Irish or Italian people who were marginalized at one point in history but who have attained whiteness and, by definition, power.

Ok, now, let's add that piping hot bowl of soup to this juggling act. As we select children's literature for the classroom, we can ask ourselves some important questions: How is this book going to act as a learning opportunity for students? Why is this text going to be part of the literacy or social studies curriculum? Does this book meet the curricular goals? (Having a "diverse books" basket in our classroom library is not the goal here. We are not going to separate #OwnVoice books to their own ghetto as if they are a separate curriculum.) Every decision we make about children's literature in our classrooms and schools must underscore this incredibly important idea—*The stories by and about marginalized people are worthy of study.*

Because representations of race and other marginalized identities are complex and interlaced with the nuances of experience, there is a need for a myriad of stories, told by a wide array of people, to bring a clearer view of that community into focus. Reading children's literature with the care and scrutiny that it deserves means paying attention to various textual and visual cues.

GETTING JUDGEY

When thinking about a book—any book you include in the curriculum—you need to think about the images and what they convey. You need to think about what the words say *and* how they interact with the images. Then you need to think about the quality of the representation and how it fits into the curriculum and how the text selections work together over the course of the literary menu the students have in front of them. It's a lot. Take a breath. Let's look at some books to help us along this journey.

Did you ever read *The Monster at the End of This Book, Starring Lovable, Furry Old Grover* (1971)? (I know it isn't an #OwnVoice book, but it will be a helpful place to start.) Right from the cover, even before you've opened the book, Grover is sharing his reading experience with the reader by asking questions directly and sharing his own interpretations of what is happening. As Grover discovers and makes sense of the text, the reader is doing the same. Throughout the book he looks at and talks directly to the reader—in some places he even pleads with the reader to realize the folly of turning the pages because "THERE IS A MONSTER AT THE END OF THE BOOK!!!" and Grover is "scared of Monsters!!!". It is the ultimate in narrative trickery because it's true—there is a monster. He, himself, is the monster at the end of the book. Grover is telling you, warning you, the reader, about himself.

But, what makes this classic picture book work? Why is this a perennial favorite, and what literacy work is it doing with the children who read it? First off, the reader feels included because Grover is having a peer-to-peer conversation. The way Grover looks at the reader, the way he asks direct questions to the reader (breaking the fourth wall), the way the illustrations and text (as part of the illustrations) add to and enforce what he is saying. All these elements invite the reader to share and co-create the experience.

The combination of words (a direct conversation with the reader) and illustrations (a main character, Grover, that gazes out of the page, directly into the reader's eyes) invites the reader to be an active participant in the story. This absurdly simple book works in ways that still amaze me. And what is the book teaching? Here is a *brief* list:

- Print awareness
- Vocabulary building (using words in concert with images to build word understanding)
- Tone and voice (using font, color, and text placement to highlight Grover's emotional state)
- Predicting (what happens with each page turn?)
- Interpretation (what does the reader think versus what Grover is telling us?)

The Monster at the End of This Book is immensely re-readable because of the combination of exciting images, the sophistication of breaking the fourth wall, and the absolute star power of Grover. Additionally, the emotional stakes are so high for both the reader and for Grover. Suspense builds page after page as Grover warns the reader against turning the next page and the reader ignores his pleas. I am sure some folks are going to say I am going too far, but this book shows an implicit message that monsters, as a group, are bad and that Grover knows this about them. Throughout the book Grover is panicked about getting to the end, where the monster is located, and he wants us to share his fear. He doesn't understand why we, the readers, keep turning the page. As adult readers, away from the fun of the overly dramatic reactions to progressing through the book, we need to ask, why is he so afraid? Why is he doing everything in his power *not* to confront the monster?

It could be that Grover is showing internalized fear of his own identity as a monster. Maybe even denial that he is a monster because, again, Grover sees monsters as threats. At the end of the book when he realizes he is the monster, the relief and surprise are palatable. Grover realizes there is no reason to be afraid of the monster at the end of the book—there is no reason for his internalized fear. He finds his reaction, his internalized fear, embarrassing. This is a fabulous entry point for kids into exploring self-acceptance and, eventually, love of self.

Now, instead of a fictional identity (monsters), let's start looking across real marginalized identities and how those identities are represented by authors and illustrators who are in and outside those communities. When we do this work, it is helpful to lean on others who have already thought deeply about the ways people see others and are seen by others. For instance, I often use Holly Johnson's "reader-viewer" connection to focus on the ways characters are positioned within the reading experience (Johnson 2019). Johnson writes that positioning the character's eye gaze toward the reader can change the experience of reading a picture book from passive voyeurism to active and invited reader participation. This lens also gives us a way to understand the ways marginalized characters and narratives are told and positioned. Do they have the power to tell the story in the ways that they want? Are the characters in charge of the story, or are they merely objects being positioned for the reader's consumption? To do this kind of analysis, you have to think of the book as the character's reality; their gaze gives us, the reader who is sitting just outside that reality, a clue as to their mental state and their awareness, their willingness and cooperation to have their story told, and to have some say in what is shared, and what is withheld. After all, when we have the power to tell the story we want to tell, it is truly our story. Using Grover as a first example, we see that from the first instance—the cover—his eyes gaze toward the reader, thus making it a more connected reading experience where we are invited to participate and not relegated to simple passive voyeurism.

Are the characters in charge of the story, or are they merely objects being positioned for the reader's consumption?

Authors and illustrators have the choice to see their characters either as whole people with complex communities, cultures, and histories, or as powerless caricatures. As we continue in this chapter, let's consider how using Johnson's "reader-viewer" lens can help us better understand and choose picture books for our classrooms.

WHO'S LOOKING? WHO'S BEING SEEN?

The ways marginalized people are presented to children matter, as award-winning author Jacqueline Woodson states much more eloquently than I ever could. In her *Horn Book* piece, "Who Can Tell My Story?" (1998), Jacqueline Woodson addresses who holds the power of representation:

> As a black person, it is easy to tell who has and who has not been inside 'my house.' Some say there is a move by people of color to keep whites from writing about us, but this isn't true. This movement isn't about white people, it's about people of color. We want the chance to tell our own stories, to tell them honestly and openly.

Woodson expresses the frustration that many people feel at seeing the call for stories about marginalized people answered by those who are the most privileged. And, to be clear, she is not asserting that writing from outside a group is impossible. She is arguing that the author should have first-hand, long-term, intimate knowledge of the people about which they write. This includes their history, their language, their community. In other words, the author needs to have real *insider* knowledge. If not, they are just another tourist, an *outsider,* reporting out existing stereotypes that they entered with and are using to reaffirm long standing, wrong-headed notions. Authors and illustrators working as cultural insiders often represent their characters differently than outsiders. This can be difficult to pin-point in detail or in ways that are teachable. The best I can do is provide examples that my students will recognize and, probably, never forget. Please remember, I teach adults (pre- and in-service teachers) so these are examples from books written by men for adult audiences, featuring their tourist view of women. And while we'll start here with examples from adult literature, as we proceed throughout this chapter, we'll find that these outsider tourist views are just as present in children's literature.

- **From *The Witches of Eastwick* (1984) by John Updike**
  "...and she had to sit on the toilet some minutes waiting for the pee to come. Men, they were able to conjure it up immediately, that was one of their powers. That thunderous splashing as they stood lordly above the bowl. **Everything about them was more direct, their insides weren't the maze women's were, for the pee to find its way through.**"

- **From *The Marriage Plot* (2011) by Jeffrey Eugenides**
  "When she'd stopped crying, Madeleine composed herself before the mirror. Her skin looked blotchy. **Her breasts, of which she was normally proud, had withdrawn into themselves, as if depressed.**"

There are more—just look up "men writing women badly" and you will spend a long weekend being shocked and completely unsurprised. And don't get me started on the ways women's bodies are depicted in comics—especially superhero comics. Just go to the now defunct (but always available) Tumblr page "The Hawkeye Initiative" where artists put men in the same costumes and poses that women have been in for years.

While these examples are hilarious in their vapid stupidity, there is also an insidiousness to the idea that men represent women as alien beings who are so desperately different, so incredibly *not* human. And this is it. The ease of which authors can dehumanize characters who are different from themselves, who are not familiar to them, leads to characters that affirm racist, sexist, homophobic, and ableist ideas. Readers should be attentive to the differences in how characters and communities are portrayed and when there is a question—do some research. What are the people in that community saying? How would someone who is being written about in that way feel? Is that character whole and complex with an imagined life off the page, or are they simply there for you, the reader, to consume?

CONSUMING AND THE EFFECTS OF THE WHITE GAZE

Novelist Toni Morrison often addressed the importance of literary criticism in books, lectures, and interviews. One phenomenon she addressed directly in the documentary, *The Pieces I Am* (Greenfield-Sanders 2019), is the "white gaze", an idea especially important when thinking about representation. Morrison explained white gaze as the feeling of having a white man sitting on her shoulder and criticizing everything she wrote. The result, as Morrison puts it, is Black authors feeling "as though our lives have no meaning and no depth without the white gaze". I look at her body of work and think that the very idea that an author like Toni Morrison would feel that some imagined white man was the arbiter of literary worth seems ludicrous given her lauded career. And that is the point. Black women working against that feeling, against the knowledge that whiteness is what everything else is judged against, is a radical action. And for readers, working against the familiar, friendly, and preen-worthy stories where whiteness is the hero is also a radical act you need to take for your students.

Let's take a look at the ways white children's book authors/illustrators and Black children's authors/illustrators create characters of color and the ways those characters interact with the reader. Specifically, are the authors and illustrators simply creating characters that perform for the white, male, hetero, abled gaze? Are we, the audience, taking the place of that white man on Morrison's shoulder and measuring everything against our expectations of whiteness? Are we, the audience, sitting in judgment, simply using and consuming the characters' story without consent, simply for our pleasure. Is the reader welcomed as a participant in the story or instead encouraged to objectify the characters? These are important questions because throughout the history of the United States, marginalized communities have been objectified and consumed. In "real life" and on the pages of books, people from marginalized groups have been treated as *something* to be used and discarded—and this habitual way of viewing literature requires intentional resistance from readers.

Is the reader welcomed as a participant in the story or instead encouraged to objectify the characters?

We are going to take a little field trip into picture books, so buckle-up, people! We are going to start with that old chestnut, *The Snowy Day*, comparing it with the more recent picture book, *Hair Love*. After that, well, let's just say ... things are going to get real.

WRITING ABOUT: *THE SNOWY DAY* BY EZRA JACK KEATS

The Snowy Day (1962), a Caldecott award-winning picture book, written and illustrated by Ezra Jack Keats, is a beloved story that has never gone out of print. You may have fond memories of having a trusted caregiver read this story to you as a young child, or seeing the animated story in class, or even more recently reading about the US Postal Service releasing a special stamp that celebrated the story (2017). In no way do we want to minimize those feelings and experiences, nor do we want to take away the historical importance of having a book for children published in 1962 that recognized and humanized Black boys. But, did it? Or, did a white man (Keats) present a Black boy as if he was a zoo animal on view for a voyeuristic white audience?

On the first page of the book we, the reader, find ourselves in Peter's bedroom while he is asleep, and we witness him wake up and look outside at the freshly fallen snow. Next, we see him sit up in his pajamas looking outside, seemingly unaware of our presence in his room (Figure 4.1).

Just think about that for a second. Why are we (the readers) there? What rights do we have to be looking on as a child sleeps? Are we part of his family? Have we been invited in? What is the story about how *we* got there? Nothing? Ok, we will move on.

The omniscient narrator tells us how Peter is feeling, what he sees, and what it all means. Next, we see Peter on the street, and we are once again peering at him from above, our eyes drawn in the direction that he is looking. He remains unaware of our witnessing as he goes about his exploration of the snow in the city streets. We watch as he climbs hills,

FIGURE 4.1
A spread from *The Snowy Day* in which Peter looks out his bedroom window to the snow.

makes snowmen, gets pummeled by snowballs thrown by older kids, and finally heads home. When he gets home, we watch as his mother undresses him, getting him out of his wet clothes, and, still, the narrator controls what we, the readers, know.

Finally, as the day and the book come to a close, we watch as Peter bathes, seeing him in profile again as he is unaware of our presence. This section where we witness Peter bathing is the epitome of objectification. Can you imagine being naked in the bath after a long day and there is a group of strangers staring down at you, listening in on your thoughts? Keats has created a tableau in which Peter, a Black boy, has no control over his body or mind and we, a predominantly white readership, are invited by the white author to take what we want for ourselves.

As an example of a book written by an outsider, *The Snowy Day* is not a harmful depiction of a Black boy. And yet, Keats uses his whiteness to gain access to the story of a Black boy without Peter giving us permission to be there. We, the reader, participate in objectifying Peter into any Black child with no real idea of his home, his family, his life. Instead, he is there for our amusement and consumption.

In contrast, how does a story written and illustrated by insiders change the way we are invited into the experience?

WRITTEN BY: *HAIR LOVE* BY MATTHEW CHERRY AND ILLUSTRATED BY VASHTI HARRISON

Hair Love (2019), written by Matthew Cherry and illustrated by Vashti Harrison, is a picture book as well as an Oscar-winning short film. This is a story about a Black girl and her father, written by a Black man and illustrated by a Black woman. The book begins, just as *The Snowy Day* does, in a child's bedroom. But, in *Hair Love*, unlike *The Snowy Day*, the main character Zuri is both the protagonist and the narrator, "My name is Zuri, and I have hair that has a mind of its own." By Zuri directly addressing us she is showing the reader that she is aware of our presence and that we are invited into the story. And, Zuri gets a chance to introduce us to her hair, almost as if it is another character (Figure 4.2).

FIGURE 4.2
Zuri from *Hair Love* introduces herself to the reader directly.

As the book progresses we, once again, see a Black child in the bathroom. The difference is that this time Zuri is fully dressed in her nightgown and slippers, sitting on a stool, looking at an iPad. We are at her level while she faces us, her eyes wide. There is nothing secret or invasive in this scene. Zuri addresses us, the readers, as she is fully aware of her circumstances, her actions, and our presence. As the story of Zuri, her hair, and her dad progresses, we are able to share the love and triumph she feels because she has provided us with the invitation to be there.

> We are at her level while she faces us, her eyes wide.

Also, as *not* a Black person, I love that this book is a great *window* book for me. I know so very little about Black hairstyles, and this book does a great job of referencing and illustrating an array of styles. I learned so much! And, we must keep in mind that hair is a political statement in our country. In this way, the author and illustrator's work allows for this book to be both reflective of Black experiences, and instructive of those same experiences for non-Black readers. It is both an intimate view of an important day, and a shared experience between the reader and the character.

But, but, but—you might want to argue—*The Snowy Day* is a "product of the times". Surely, *Hair Love* is the new normal now that we have more Black people writing their own stories ... right? Right?!? RIGHT?

Oh, so very wrong. Let's look at two very modern-day books that feature young gender expansive characters of color.

WRITTEN ABOUT AND WRITTEN BY: RACE AND GENDER IN *JULIÁN* AND *AIDAN*

I want to extend Morrison's idea of the white gaze to the normative gaze—a white, straight, cis, abled gaze. So, just as Keats wrote and illustrated from his white, male perspective, Jessica Love presents us with *Julián is a Mermaid* (2018) from her white, straight, cis perspective. This familiar *normative gaze* is one reason for the absolute adoration of this book, along with the awards heaped upon it. The book is artistically gorgeous—watercolors and ink splash across the heavy, textured brown paper giving it a vibrancy that is easy to appreciate. This picture book is just like *Snowy Day* in that it is an intimate and uninvited view of a boy of color. But, unlike Peter whose actions are public and expected, Julián tries to keep his actions private and hidden away from prying eyes.

And (this is an important "and" so I am going to write it again) **AND** just like *Snowy Day* is not really Peter's story, this isn't Julián's story. This book is the imagined story of a white, cis, straight woman who brings her identity to the work, and with her identity comes her outsider's intrusive gaze. This is going to be a complicated walk through the book so bear with me.

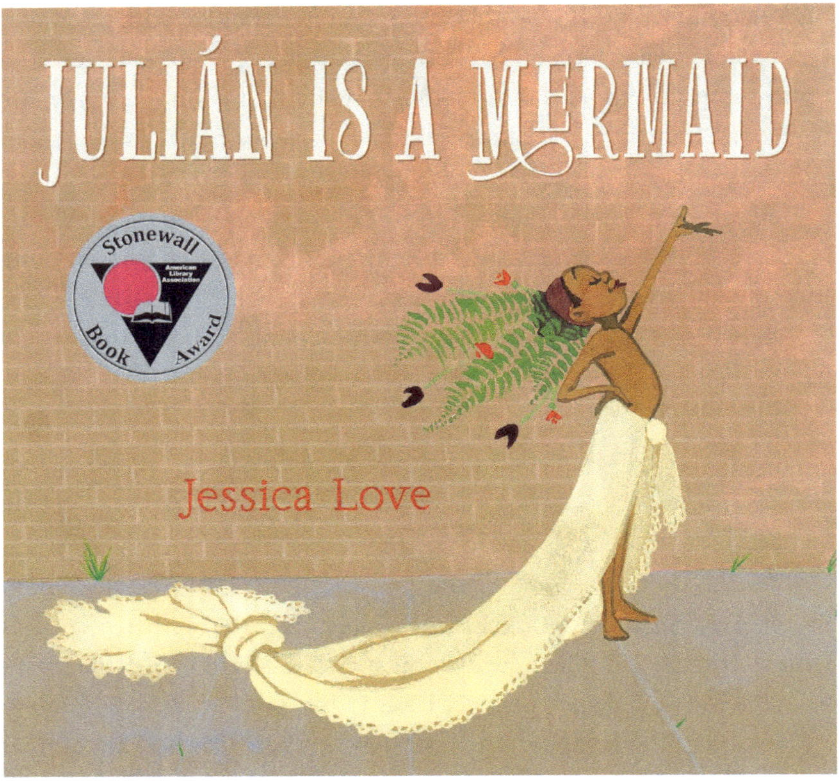

FIGURE 4.3
The cover of *Julián is a Mermaid* by Jessica Love.

The picture book cover (Figure 4.3) shows Julián, who I read as Afro Latino, in his femme and fabulous presentation with his head thrown back, his back arched, one hand on his pre-pubescent hip, and the other outstretched above his head, reaching. Perhaps most importantly, he is outside, standing against a brick wall, on a sidewalk for all to see. This sets the reader up to think that he is out and proud. But, in fact, Julián is not out. You see, he dreams of being a beautiful, femme mermaid and he, at this very young age, knows this is something he has to hide. The book begins with the lines "This is a boy named Julián. And this is his abuela. And those are some mermaids." The mermaids in question are a group of drag queens bedecked in flowing aqua dresses, big hair, big earrings, and perfectly on point makeup. Julián is enamored with them while his abuela shows no interest.

We see him dreaming of becoming a mermaid (which includes him stripping down to his underwear) on the subway and then he walks home with his abuela, passing folks doing summer things like playing in water from a fire hydrant. When Julián and his abuela get home she says, "I'm going to take a bath, you be good." As she leaves, Julián stands, leaning against a chest of drawers, his feet crossed, knees together, hand behind his back and his chin slightly down, and a slight smile on his face, his eyes a little closed, as if he is playing at innocence.

The next page reads, "He has a good idea." Julián takes advantage of the moment of privacy to strip down to his white brief underwear and transform himself into a beautiful mermaid by wrapping a long lace tablecloth into a tail and creating a headpiece with fern fronds and flowers. In reading this book, I feel like I am trespassing on a private moment, like an unwelcome peeping Tom at the window as he takes off his clothes and stands in his underwear to begin his transformation. Julián's surprise at the appearance of his abuela during his metamorphosis is one indicator that he was in a private space, having private thoughts and experiences. This is not Love's story to tell, but she is successfully mirroring the expectations of the normative gaze and creating a sense of the familiar for readers who share Love's identity.

Again, Woodson's plea stands out to me when reading any book written by an outsider, "We want the chance to tell our own stories, to tell them honestly and openly" (1998). And, I am wary of the comfort the normative, in this case white, straight, and cis, gaze provides in lieu of an actual authentic representation of marginalized identities. The need for an insider view seems counterintuitive to many, so I want to provide a counter narrative to the familiar and objectifying representation of Julián by Jessica Love, and instead walk through *When Aidan Became a Brother* (2019) written by Kyle Lukoff and illustrated by Kaylani Juanita. Let's start with the cover again (Figure 4.4).

On this cover, the title is a banner and there are celebratory sparkles raining down on the family. We see Aidan and his father smiling and looking at us, the readers, as Aidan's pregnant mother kisses him on the head. This cover image does so much to set the stage for the reader—we are invited into a celebration with the Black family. But the first

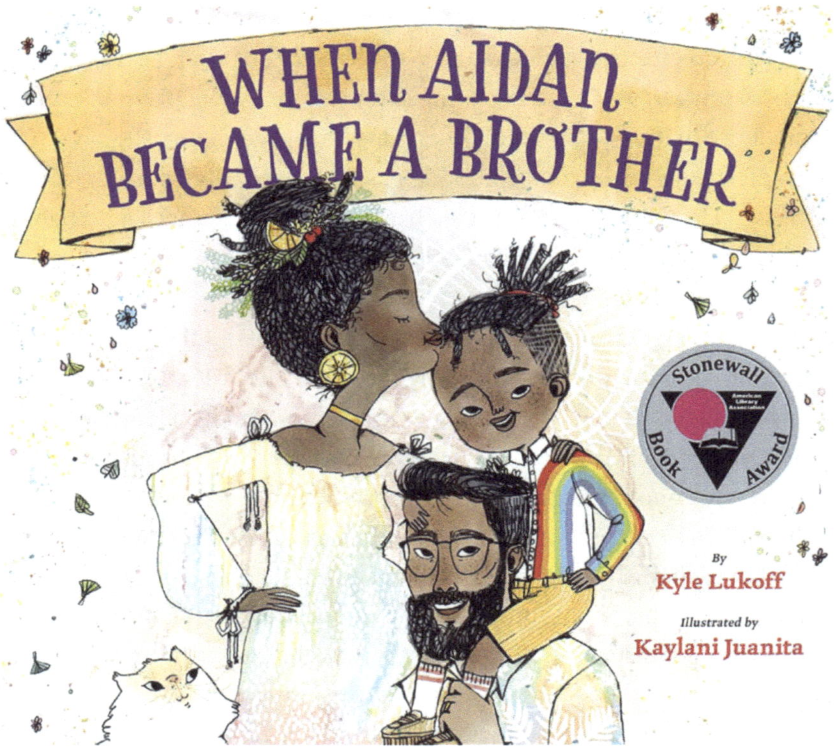

FIGURE 4.4
The cover of *When Aidan Became a Brother* written by Kyle Lukoff and illustrated by Kaylani Juanita.

page tells a very different tale. We see Aidan sitting in his very girly room, wearing a dress, his natural hair held back with a headband but still a bit of a mess, and he looks miserable. Aidan's gaze is not exactly directed at us. Instead, he sits facing us, his body directed to the left, and his gaze directed just to the right of us, not meeting our eyes, but including us nonetheless. As the story progresses, we get to witness Aidan's struggle with his gender identity, and his parents struggle to understand what Aidan is trying to tell them. The narrator declares, Aidan "didn't feel like any kind of girl. He was really another kind of boy" (Lukoff 2019).

Later, as he sits on top of his dresser, his freshly cut hair tumbling down in little piles, he smiles at the mirror. It is incredibly important to acknowledge the politics of hair and identity in the Black community.

These elements that may not affect us (non-Black folks) must be recognized even (and especially) by those of us that are outside the community. And, while Aidan looks at himself in the mirror, we are included, looking at him as he looks at himself and at us—we share his moment of quiet triumph.

On the next page, the text names the kind of boy Aidan is—he's transgender. As the book moves forward, his family gets to know other families with trans kids, Aidan gets the room decor he wants, the clothes he is comfortable in, and the haircut that expresses his identity. All of this happens while including the reader, with his parents on full display, and a community being built around them. Aidan is not isolated. It is important to note that his body is also not on full display—unlike those of Peter and Julián. At no point do I, as an adult viewer, know what kind of underwear he wears or what he looks like in the bath. And, to be sure, there is a scene in the bath where Aidan is practicing reading and the illustrator shows the top of his head (in a shower cap), his elbow, and his hands holding a book. Even in this intimate bathing space, Aidan's privacy and body remain his own (Figure 4.5).

FIGURE 4.5
An illustration from *When Aidan Became a Brother* that shows him in the bath, but with his privacy and bodily autonomy in place.

And keep in mind, all this happened in the first eleven pages! That's because this is not an "issue book". This is not the story that stops at Aidan's trans identity. Instead, the story is about (checks notes) *When Aidan Became a Brother*—oh, how I love a sneaky title. The rest of the book centers on how Aidan and his family prepare to welcome a new baby into the family. How Aidan helps his parents give the new baby the gender-inclusive experience he wished he had—from baby names to room decor to gender reveal. It is as much a mirror for gender expansive kids (and adults) as it is for us cis folks who are just stumbling around trying our best.

In choosing books that we offer children in our classrooms, which books we read aloud, which books we celebrate, it is critical that we slow down to consider the complex and multi-layered issues of representation. We must ask, how are marginalized, multi-faceted identities represented through the characters on the pages? And who gets to tell their stories? The answers are not always easy. We can begin by choosing stories created by those who have deep knowledge and experiences of the communities and identities they represent on the pages of the books they make.

We must ask, how are marginalized, multi-faceted identities represented through the characters on the pages?

CHAPTER 5

WHO'S AFRAID OF THE BIG BANNED BOOK?

THE POLITICS OF CHILDREN'S LITERATURE

When I get to the part of the semester where my teacher education students and I talk about banned and challenged books, the students always ask great questions such as:

- Who is actually responsible for the bans and challenges?
- Wait, what about the first amendment?
- If a book is banned in schools, is it still for sale?
- What happens if teachers ignore a ban?
- Ok, but freedom of speech????

In the ever-changing world of book bans, challenges, and book-related lawsuits, there's always more to learn, so I invite you into this chapter with a spirit of investigation so that ultimately, we can advocate for and work toward change. There are still some things we might not be able to figure out, but that is the nature of the world. Sometimes things are just weird.

To begin this chapter, we are going to learn a little history, which can be a humbling teacher. Mary McCarthy said, "We are the hero of our own story", and I think that goes for both individuals and societies.

No one wants to tell a story where we end up as the horse's ass. Instead, we weave events together to make everyone else look like unwashed rabble while we stand apart in our shiny suit of armor. Americans, especially, often hold the unprovable belief that we are the best country in the world. Why? What stories have been told that make us believe, contrary to all objective measures, historical events, and current day issues, that we are #1 [insert huge foam finger].

I mean, come on! We have huge racial disparities in infant and maternal mortality rates; one of the highest incarceration rates in the world; higher poverty rates than other industrialized countries; crumbling infrastructure; we are one of the top three emissions contributors globally; and our education system is deeply hurting. We are a country that is *literally* built on the economic choice to repeatedly enslave humans, along with the temerity to deny the long-lasting consequences of those actions.

So, we, both as individuals and as a society, might be the heroes of our own story, but don't forget, we are often unreliable narrators. So, what does this history have to do with banned books? Let's dig in.

BANNED, CHALLENGED, AND CENSORED, OH MYYYYYY...

The first question that usually comes up around banned books is "WTF? What do you mean books are banned in America? What about the first amendment?" The next question is often "Wait, what's the difference between banning, challenging, and censoring?" Let's take these questions together as a group—like a stench of internet skunks.

America has a long history of banning, challenging, and censoring ideas, actions, people, and books. Heck, even before we were a country we were banning stuff that we didn't like. According to Colleen Connolly (2023) writing for the Smithsonian, the first banned book in the US was a pamphlet, *The New English Canaan* by Thomas Morton, printed in Amsterdam and distributed in and around Plymouth Colony in 1637. In this pamphlet, Morton criticized the hierarchical power structure of the puritans and denounced the genocide of Indigenous people. The Puritans, somewhat unsurprisingly, banned the text and labeled it a "scurrilous book". Massachusetts coming in hot with speaking truth to power and immediately getting shut down. If you want to read more about the history of book bans, may I suggest:

- "The History of Book Bans—and Their Changing Targets—in the U.S." by Erin Blakemore (2024)
- "Manuscripts Don't Burn: A Timeline of Literary Censorship, Destruction, and Liberation" by PEN America (2023)
- *That Librarian: The Fight Against Book Banning in America* by Amanda Jones (2024)

Let's start at the beginning. The first amendment was ratified in 1791 and states that:

> **Congress shall make no law** respecting an establishment of religion, or prohibiting the free exercise thereof; or **abridging the freedom of speech**, or of the press; or the right of the people peaceably to assemble, and to petition the government for a redress of grievances.

And, they have held to that. Read it carefully. The first amendment only applies to the federal government censoring and banning acts of speech (and we can argue books are the *ultimate* speech act). But in Board of Education v. Pico (1982) the United States Supreme Court ruled that "the right to receive ideas is a necessary predicate to the recipient's meaningful exercise of his own rights of speech, press, and political freedom" ("Island Trees Sch. Dist. v. Pico by Pico, 457 US 853" 1982). Although the ruling was a close one—five to four—the Court ruled that ideas, even ideas people don't like, cannot be banned from school libraries simply because they are unpopular. Instead, the Court stated that libraries are special bastions of free speech and press.

Currently, folks who are banning and challenging books are trying a new tactic that goes something like this:

- I am a taxpayer in this municipal area, therefore
- my taxes pay for the materials in the libraries and schools

- and so, I have the right to say what should or should not be present in the contents of the libraries and schools
- Oh, and my favorite part of this syllogism from hell: I think this book is so incredibly heinous that not only do I want to keep it out of my child's hands but I want to keep it out of *all* children's hands, no matter if any other adult (parent, teacher, librarian) agrees with me or not

Just for clarification—a challenged book is one that, well, has been challenged. Some adult walks into a library or a school and states that they want (and I paraphrase here) "this piece of trash off the shelf". Libraries and schools usually have some sort of policy and process for challenging books, and it usually includes the book being removed from general circulation for review. Once a challenge is made, the book goes through a review process—which are all different—and if the book is deemed unworthy for public consumption it is removed from the school or library collection. And, since this is all local, remember a ban only reaches the limits of the municipal border. If you have the money, you can still purchase the book. If the book is banned or challenged, it is (temporarily or permanently) not available in the library or the school.

WHO GETS BANNED?

There are distinct topics that get banned most frequently and which ones they are isn't even a tiny bit surprising. According to PEN America's report (2024), the most common trait about the books we are removing from schools and libraries are those that feature Black, Indigenous, and People of Color (BIPOC) (44 percent of all books removed) and Lesbian, Gay, Bi, Trans, Queer, and Intersex characters and authors (39 percent of all books removed), with the majority of books being banned geared toward YA audiences. But that doesn't mean picture books have been left alone. Books like *And Tango Makes Three* by Peter Parnell, *The Family Book* (2003) by Todd Parr, *When Aidan Became a Brother* by Kyle Lukoff, and *One Day in June* by Tourmaline are some of the more frequently banned or challenged books for young readers. Wanna guess what the perceived issue is?

And let's be clear. All of these books share some important elements. They are all picture books that feature LGBTQIA+ characters in age-appropriate ways. But, that's just it. Many folks in the US do not believe there *is* an "age-appropriate" way to feature LGBTQIA+ characters.

Many folks in the US do not believe there *is* an "age-appropriate" way to feature LGBTQIA+ characters.

I'll let you all in on a little secret from my own life. Our sons, and all our sons' friends, and all our sons' friends' parents and teachers knew they had two moms. In fact, these kids talked about it, openly. One snowy day our older son (I'll call him Jake, because that is his name) had a few friends over for sledding, games, and hot chocolate. The kids were probably eight years old at the time, and I overheard the following conversation:

Kid 1: *You have two moms?*

Jake: *Yeah.*

Kid 2: *At the same time?*

Jake: *Yeah.*

Kid 1: *My cousin has two moms, but only one at a time. (I think he was talking about having a blended family.)*

Jake: *Nope. I've got a mom and a mimi. All the time.*

Kid 1: *Wow. That's a lot of moms.*

Jake: *Yeah. There's a lot of rules.*

And then they turned their attention to playing Minecraft. That was it. A couple of third graders talking about lesbianism on a snowy day as I (an actual lesbian) made snacks and monitored them from afar. No one was swallowed by a demon mound, there was no rending of clothes or gnashing of teeth. Instead, the kids who frequented our home drank my hot chocolate or iced herbal tea, and socialized with our family and had the chance to experience our family's *big-fat gay agenda* which primarily included:

- Getting more sleep
- Keeping bleeding and yelling to a minimum
- Eating more good healthy food than processed food
- Picking up Legos, cleats, and other shoes to avoid bleeding and yelling
- Putting dishes in the dang dishwasher and rolls of toilet paper on the actual freakin' spindle thing! What is so hard about that?
- Not being jerks

In other words, my sons' friends had the opportunity to see up close that our family of two moms was, in many ways, similar to the families in which they lived. Books, too, provide these windows into families that are similar and different to one's own lived experiences. However, if books about BIPOC or LGBTQIA+ families are banned or are otherwise disappeared from the shelves, children miss out on these chances to think and talk about what makes a family.

Books, too, provide these windows into families that are similar and different to one's own lived experiences.

WHY DOES BOOK BANNING MATTER?

In 2021 high school teacher Matthew Hawn was fired for teaching about whiteness in his "Contemporary Issues in America" class in Sullivan County, Tennessee. Specifically, he was fired over assigning Ta-Nehisi Coates' article "The First White President". Eventually, the state court ordered Hawn to be reinstated with back pay (Dennis 2024).

In 2022 Oklahoma teacher Summer Boismier shared a QR code for the Brooklyn Public Library's catalogue of banned books with her high school students. New York City libraries allow anyone to get an e-library card to access their online catalogue of audio and e-books. Boismier's teaching license was revoked by the state of Oklahoma (Lathan 2024).

In 2023 Katie Rinderle, a teacher in Georgia, sat in her fifth-grade classroom and read *My Shadow is Purple* (2022) by Scott Stuart. This picture book is about a gender expansive kid who does not belong within the gender binaries, and who stays true to themself. Katie Rinderle was fired on June 6, 2023 specifically for reading this book (Rinderle 2023).

Teachers are on the front lines of a new culture war. They are fighting against unjust book bans and challenges that overwhelmingly target the stories of BIPOC and LGBTQIA+ folks whose stories are being taken off shelves in classrooms and libraries, removed from lessons, and yanked out of the hands of students.

And make no mistake, there are messages being sent by these actions. When a student sees their family, culture, religion, their story simply omitted, it leaves them with the understanding that they themselves do not belong. When authorities literally keep you and your peers from learning about groups of people and individuals, it hurts everyone. It keeps everyone ignorant and scared of difference, and in some cases, of themselves. Many educators, concerned for their livelihood, are seeing these actions across the country as warning signs and are acting accordingly by preemptively removing books that may be deemed harmful.

More and more states are implementing restrictions on the types of books that can be taught and carried in the libraries. These laws can be extremely general, like Texas's Senate Bill 3 (passed in 2021) which states that no curriculum material can be used if it causes any student discomfort based on the student's race or gender (Lopez 2021). Or, Texas Senate Bill 13 (passed in 2024 and put into effect in 2025) which puts school boards, not librarians, in charge of which books will be allowed in school libraries (Runnels 2025). Other states are following suit, passing laws impacting books in schools and libraries. For example:

- Utah has created a statewide "No-Read List". Utah's HB 29 has a clause that sets a state-wide ban in motion if three school districts or two school districts and five charter schools determine a book contains "objective sensitive material", as defined by the legislature (Markham and LaFrance 2024). So far nineteen (and counting) novels have made the list

- Missouri passed SB 775 in 2022 which makes it a criminal act to provide "explicit sexual material" to students which seems like a terrific plan until you realize the effect. Because the restrictions are vague and the punishments are extreme (fines and jail) there has been a sharp increase in book removals across the state as a result of these laws (PEN America August 23, 2023)
- And then there is Florida, the ultimate "hold my beer" state. Their legislature passed the "Don't Say Gay" bill (HB 1557) in 2022 and expanded it with HB 1069 in 2023. Together these laws basically erase LBGTQIA+ people from all aspects of school life affecting all curricula in grades K-12. These laws make it easier to ban books across the state but stop short of creating state-wide banned lists (PEN America August 23, 2023)

All these laws, and probably more to come, amount to keeping people, cultures, and history hidden with the express purpose of protecting whiteness, straightness, and cisness.

HOW DO WE START? TAKING ACTION AGAINST BOOK BANS

You can't fix the world. You probably don't have access to lots of power in the federal government, or even your state government. Instead, think locally. Where can your voice reach? Who can you affect? What is your personal sphere of influence? Start there.

- Educate yourself on your local political landscape by attending a school board meeting or town/city council meeting. Most meet monthly, and many meet on Zoom. These meetings swing between sleep-inducing boredom and an absolute wild ride. There is no middle
- Research the process for challenging (or approving) books in your school district or library. Again, attend a meeting, especially if they are addressing book challenges
- Ask your local librarian how to request books to be added to the collection and then use that process to request amazing books

- Ask your book group, church group, friend group, or random parents at the bake sale to request books that feature LGBTQIA+ and BIPOC characters and history be added to the library collection at school
- If you want to go to the next level, look into legislation affecting your state. Is there a "Right to Read" bill? Are there bills being voted on that are designed to restrict who can be talked about or taught in schools? Take action and call and write to your representatives
- Have conversations with your students about book banning/challenging books. Highlight all the books in your classroom or in the library that are actively being banned and challenged in some areas. Kids love a banned/challenged book

CHAPTER 6

WAIT! WHAT THE HELL AM I SUPPOSED TO DO WITH ALL OF THIS?

I often end my college classes with a sort of summary of all the things we have read and talked about. Something like,

> Here's the deal: genres are ridiculous, nonsensical categories that do as much good as harm. Don't ever forget they are made up for convenience sake—so we can speak in a common language. But, sometimes the most interesting and exciting books are those that cross, mix or completely ignore genre restrictions and instead, show us a new kind of story.

I'm going to try this kind of summary for this entire book. Let's see if it helps! The idea of this book is to offer a combination of technical knowledge about children's literature *and* opportunities for building a more complex critical consciousness about the books that are made for and shared with kids. The technical stuff is like the ABCs—once you know them, they're there for you to use and build on in multiple ways. The critical consciousness stuff is more complex, nuanced, messy, and really requires the reader to do a lot of self-reflection. This work comes with an explicit ask—learn more, do better.

MISTAKES WERE MADE

My message is clear—*Mistakes are the norm.* Try your best, be aware, and be humble enough to say, "Ooohhh, yeah, my bad. Sorry. Let me try that again." Do reparative work and do better in the future. That is all we can ask of each other and of ourselves.

Next, it's complicated. Race, gender, class, religion, ability status, and all the rest. These categories are all messy social constructs with *loads* of baggage. At first glance, we may not recognize the role they play within children's literature and publishing. And, when we say they are social constructs, this means they are both made up not real things *and* the most important things in our society. Both of these ideas can be true at the same time. Remember, it's complicated.

Also, no identity is experienced or expressed in isolation, nor is there a single way to express one's identity. I am a cis Latina lesbian all of the time. I can't pull out one bit and leave the rest. I also cannot experience or truly understand what I am not. I have to rely on others to help and I have to remind myself to keep vigilant because the stories I was told are the stories I know to be true—even if those stories are 100 percent wrong. Also, there is no singular experience or story or way of being that represents the entirety of a community. There is as much variability within a community as there is between communities.

> There is no singular experience or story or way of being that represents the entirety of a community.

Furthermore (and this one is really hard), the experience of marginalization is not transferable. I wish it were, but there is far too much evidence to the contrary. That means white gay men do not automatically get a pass for being racist and misogynistic; lesbians are often transphobic; Black communities have a history of anti-LGBTQIA+ actions; and ableism is alive and well across all communities. We all carry awful societal "truths" around with us because we are born and raised and educated in *this* society. No one gets out clean.

I want to stand up and say, I am not immune to oppressive, essentializing ideas. Remember the section earlier in this book about *When Aidan Became*

FIGURE 6.1
Aidan keeps his hair dry in the bath in *When Aidan Became a Brother*.

a Brother? I wanted to write about one image—out of three on that particular page—where Aidan is in the tub practicing reading (Figure 6.1). I know Aidan is wearing something on his hair to keep it dry, but I wasn't sure what to call it. It looked like a bonnet but I can't imagine a bonnet being worn in the tub. My understanding of a bonnet, from the Black and Afro Latine community, is that it is a cover for your hair, usually made out of soft satin that protects hair from tangling, flattening, and drying out while sleeping. Again, my very *not* Black understanding of a bonnet was based on what I've heard and social media conversations.

So here I am writing about a Black trans kid wearing what looks to me like a bonnet in the bathtub. Yup. I am out of my element. *Way* out. I mean, is it called a bonnet? A bath bonnet? It can't be the same soft satin because that doesn't make sense—or does it? I don't know. Maybe satin is water repellent? Maybe that's not the point? Maybe it's used to protect hair from the humidity of the tub?

As I was writing, I was getting lost in my head and spiraling. "Why am I even writing this? What the hell do I know about Black trans boys? WHAT AM I EVEN DOING HERE????" I let myself panic for a minute, got a spoonful of peanut butter and a glass of water—I was probably low on protein and water is always a good idea. And then I texted a couple of Black and Latine colleagues (no white folk!) asking them, "What would you call the head covering this kid is wearing?" and I attached the image in Figure 6.1. I got a few different answers. Clearly not a consensus. Panic again. More water.

I needed more answers to find a consensus. Was there a consensus? I mean, the very act of trying to find consensus was one built on the essentializing idea that *all* Black folks thought the same thing. More peanut butter was clearly needed.

I eventually went to Facebook and posted the following:

> Attention BLACK and AFRO LATINE PEOPLE * ONLY
>
> Would you refer to what this child wearing as:
>
> **A.** Shower cap
>
> **B.** Bath bonnet
>
> **C.** Other ... please specify
>
> *If you wear a bonnet but do not identify as Black or Afro Latine, the only reason I am restricting this is the character representation.
>
> *Also, if you are white and have a Black friend who says ... I'm. Not. Interested.

Thank you to those who responded to my post: Jerry Whitemore; Twyla Blackmond; Dhonielle Clayton; Wintre Johnson; Davena Meadows; Andrea J. Loney; Stephany Jones; Stephanie Toliver; Caysie Harvey; Marti Dumas; Michele Schmidt Moore; Hannah Gomez; Jen Brooks; Varian Johnson; TA Martin; and Keisha Smith-Carrington.

My friends and colleagues showed up for me. They took the time to support me, to guide me, and to educate me. They were kind enough to share their expertise for me to learn from and to pass on because they know I approach this work with a sense of humility, respect, care, and love. They know I am not going to assume that I know the answer—instead I am going to reach out to the community. I am not going to ask my one

Black friend. I am going to try super hard not to think that there is *one* truth. Instead, I work to be part of a committed learning community that is diverse across multiple marginalized identities.

And that is also your work too. You need to step outside your familiar community. Even when you make mistakes. Even when you worry you are messing up. Even when you need peanut butter to get through a rough moment. That work might be in real life (just do so with respect), it might be online (be careful, it's still weird out here), or it might be done by reading, listening, and watching outside your norm.

And that is also your work too. You need to step outside your familiar community.

And the best part of all of this? We are living in a time where more and more books by and about marginalized people are reaching the bookshelves. These books give us the opportunity to do this work in partnership with the amazing authors and illustrators out there who are creating great books for children. We really don't have to keep teaching the same, familiar books. We can revel in the stories coming out all the time that are worthy of a place in our classrooms and in our curriculum.

So, that's it really. Read widely, with care and humility, recognize your own identities, privileges, and areas that you need to learn more about and do that work, center the most marginalized identities, watch for sneaky familiar representations that reify existing biased tropes, be critical of social hysteria cloaked in protecting the children, and rinse and repeat forever.

RESOURCES

I want to end this book with some ideas and resources that help me, my colleagues, and my teacher-students.

Resources Focused on Children's Literature

These resources are a great way to find books that you might not come across if you aren't looking. These are given in alphabetic order.

- ***American Indians in Children's Literature*** Dr. Debbie Reese, Nambé Pueblo, provides critical analysis of Indigenous peoples in children's and YA books. You can learn a lot about how to read critically, in general, from her carefully constructed posts. Check out the Best Books section, and pay attention to the Not Recommended tag (found on the long lists of tags on the right side of the screen)

- ***Social Justice Books*** This organization has an absolute ton of up-to-date reviews. They also do the important work of providing book lists across all kinds of marginalized identities, histories, and events. They act as a consortium of book reviews so this resource is one of the first places I go to find new books
- ***We are Kidlit Collective*** Started by the amazing librarian Edith Campbell, this is a group of folks who review many children's and YA books that are written by and about BIPOC people. They spend the year collecting and critically engaging with the literature and each other to come up with the best possible summer reading list

Resources Focused on Critical Literacy Practices

- *Cultivating Genius: An Equity Framework for Culturally and Historically Responsive Literacy* by Gholdy Muhammad
- *Culturally Responsive Teaching and The Brain: Promoting Authentic Engagement and Rigor Among Culturally and Linguistically Diverse Students* by Zaretta L. Hammond
- *En Comunidad: Lessons for Centering the Voices and Experiences of Bilingual Latinx Students* by Carla España and Luz Yadira Herrera
- *Literacy Is Liberation: Working Toward Justice Through Culturally Relevant Teaching* by Kimberly N. Parker
- *Unearthing Joy: A Guide to Culturally and Historically Responsive Teaching and Learning* by Gholdy Muhammad

Resources Especially for White Women

White women have some specific work to do that can bring out some serious issues of vulnerability. Patriarchal whiteness teaches white women that they will be protected from harm if they follow and enforce the rules of compliance, conflict avoidance, and perfectionism. This is not to say that *only* white women need to do this work—it's just that overwhelming representation in education makes it astonishingly clear that we need white women to change.

According to Pew research, 89 percent of elementary teachers are women, 72 percent of middle school teachers are women, and 60 percent of secondary or high school teachers are women (Schaeffer 2024). Although I could not find stats that combine gender and race, the racial demographics are also similarly stark. The most recent numbers are from 2021 and they found 80 percent of teachers identified as white, followed by 9 percent Hispanic, 6 percent Black, 2 percent Asian American or multiracial (which is an odd combined category if you ask me), and Pacific Islander or American Indian and Alaska Native pulling less than 1 percent (Schaeffer 2024). So, really, white women are massively represented in teaching. Even as our country and classrooms become increasingly racially diverse, our teacher population remains largely white and female.

There is a *lot* for white women to unlearn about race, gender, and patriarchal values and that is not the work of this book that is focused on children's literature. Here are some resources.

BOOKS

- *White Women: Everything You Already Know About Your Own Racism and How to Do Better* by Regina Jackson and Saira Rao
- *White Tears/Brown Scars: How White Feminism Betrays Women of Color* by Ruby Hamad
- *White Evangelical Racism: The Politics of Morality in America* by Anthea Butler

PODCASTS

- NPR's *Code Switch*
- *Yo, Is This Racist?* hosted by Andre Ti and Tawney Newsome
- *Seeing White* (Season 2 of *Scene on Radio*) produced and hosted by John Biewen

Resources Especially for Younger LGBTQIA+ Folks (and All the Straights)

Again, the vast majority of teachers identify as straight. And, more importantly, LGBTQIA+ history is actively erased from almost all school curricula, so here are some places you can start learning.

BOOKS

- *A Queer History of the United States for Young People* by Richie Chevat and Michael Bronski
- *Generation Queer: Stories of Youth Organizers, Artists, and Educators* by Kimm Topping and Anshika Khullar

WATCH

- *Stonewall Uprising* by PBS American Experience
- *POSE* on Hulu

PODCASTS

- *Making Gay History* hosted by Eric Marcus
- *Daniel: Being a Double Minority in a Red State* (Season 2, Ep 4, "When You're Invisible")

APPENDIX A: LITERARY AUTOBIOGRAPHY EXERCISE

A Literary Autobiography of Books You Loved as a Child or Read in School			
How I Identify I identify as (race) ______ I identify as (gender) ______ I identify as (sexual orientation) ______			
BOOK TITLE	PROTAGONIST'S		
	RACE	GENDER	SEXUAL ORIENTATION

A note: while we have focused here on three important elements of identity—race, gender, and sexual orientation—we could also complete this same exercise considering other elements of identity including ability/disability, religion, socio-economic status, and language.

APPENDIX B: CRITICAL VISUAL LITERACY WORKSHEET

PART 1

Grab one of your "go to" picture books—one that is familiar, that you use often in your class or in your curriculum. You know the one, it's a long time favorite or an old standby because you know it better than the contents of your favorite bag. Maybe choose from the books you read at the beginning of the year or one that you use after testing is done in May and you know everyone just needs a break. Read one of those books with a critical lens and try to figure out what these books are communicating about who is worth centering, what is being communicated about these groups of people, and what you were hoping students might take away from the book into their world.

Start with the easy stuff. (Note that you may have to make some assumptions to fill this out or there may be lines you leave blank if you don't know.)

Book title ______________________________

Author ______________________________

Illustrator ______________________________

Author identity

Race ______________ Gender ______________

Sexual Orientation ____________ Religiousness ____________

Notes on Other Aspects of Identity

____

Illustrator Identity

Race ______________ Gender ______________

Sexual Orientation ____________ Religiousness ____________

Notes on Other Aspects of Identity

____

PART 2

Select a page of your chosen picture book to really focus in on. Maybe one that is a double-page spread, where there are lots of images, characters, and actions going on. You want to look at something that is complex and meaningful because that is where the author and illustrator are doing the most work to communicate with the reader.

YOU TRY IT! USING CRITICAL VISUAL LITERACY TO NOTICE AND NAME
Step 1: Chunk apart the page. If there are multiple parts of an illustration, analyze one part at a time and then repeat Steps 2–6 for each part of the illustration.
Step 2: Name who you see. Use direct language to name race, gender, sexual orientation, ability, socio-economic status, and religious affiliation.
Step 3: Notice details. Part of the exercise is to surface and challenge what we see and how we interpret that image.
Step 4: Think about the stereotypes we tell (related to what you have named in Step 2).
Step 5: Ask: How are the images aligned with or in opposition to these stereotypes? Compare the image to the stereotypes and "othering" messages.
Step 6: If, after engaging this process, we conclude that this isn't a book we want to share with children in our classrooms, **what's another book (focus on #OwnVoices) we might read instead?**

REFERENCES

Allington, Richard L. 1977. "If They Don't Read Much, How They Ever Gonna Get Good?" *Journal of Reading* 21 (1): 57–61.

Barthes, Roland. 1977. "The Death of the Author." In *Image-Music-Text*, ed. Stephen Heath. New York: Hill and Wang.

Bishop, Rudine Sims. 1990. "Windows, Mirrors, and Sliding Glass Doors. *Perspectives* 6 (3): ix–xi.

Blakemore, Erin. 2024. "The History of Book Bans—and Their Changing Targets—in the U.S." September 20. National Geographic. https://www.nationalgeographic.com/culture/article/history-of-book-bans-in-the-united-states.

Connolly, Colleen. 2023. "How America's First Banned Book Survived and Became an Anti-Authoritarian Icon." October 2. *Smithsonian Magazine*. https://www.smithsonianmag.com/history/how-americas-first-banned-book-survived-and-became-an-anti-authoritarian-icon-180982971/.

Crenshaw, Kimberlé. 1991. "Mapping the Margins: Intersectionality, Identity Politics, and Violence against Women of Color." *Stanford Law Review* 43 (6): 1241–1299.

Crenshaw, Kimberlé, et al., eds. 1995. *Critical Race Theory: The Key Writings That Formed the Movement*. New York: The New Press.

Delgado, Ricard, and Jean Stefancic. 2023. *Critical Race Theory: An Introduction*. 4th ed. New York: NYU Press.

Dennis, Angela. 2024. "Court Reinstates Tennessee Teacher Fired for Discussing Critical Race Theory." December 20. *Tennessee Lookout*. https://tennesseelookout.com/2024/12/20/court-reinstates-tennessee-teacher-fired-for-discussing-critical-race-theory/.

Dickinson, Kari. 2024. "CCBC's Diversity Statistics Show Small Changes in Number of Diverse Books for Children and Teens Published Last Year." April 3. University of Wisconsin–

Madison School of Education. https://education.wisc.edu/news/ccbcs-diversity-statistics-show-small-changes-in-number-of-diverse-books-for-children-and-teens-published-last-year/.

Dixson, Adrienne D., and Celia Rousseau Anderson. 2018. "Where Are We? Critical Race Theory in Education 20 Years Later." *Peabody Journal of Education* 93 (1): 121–131.

Duke, Nell K., Alessandra E. Ward, and P. David Pearson. 2021. "The Science of Reading Comprehension Instruction." *The Reading Teacher* 74 (6): 663–672.

Duyvis, C. (@corinneduyvis). 2015. "#OwnVoices." Twitter, September 6.

Greenfield-Sanders, Timothy (Director). 2019. Toni Morrison: *The Pieces I Am* [Film]. Magnolia Pictures.

hooks, bell. 1989. "Choosing the Margin as a Space of Radical Openness." *Framework: The Journal of Cinema and Media* 36: 15–23.

"Island Trees Sch. Dist. v. Pico by Pico, 457 US 853." 1982. US Supreme Court. https://supreme.justia.com/cases/federal/us/457/853/.

Johnson, Holly. 2019. "The Power of a Gaze: Inviting Entrée into the World of a Picturebook While Positioning a Lived Reality." In *Critical Content Analysis of Visual Images in Books for Young People*. New York: Routledge.

Jones, Amanda. 2024. *That Librarian: The Fight Against Book Banning in America*. New York: Bloomsbury.

King, Martin Luther Jr. 1968. "Remaining Awake Through a Great Revolution." March 31. National Cathedral, Washington, D.C.

Ladson-Billings, Gloria, and William F. Tate IV. 2022. "Toward a Critical Race Theory of Education." *Teachers College Record: The Voice of Scholarship in Education* 97 (1): 47–68.

Lathan, Nadia. 2024. "Oklahoma Revokes License of Teacher who Gave Class QR Code to Brooklyn Library in Book-Ban Protest." August 23. *AP Education News*. https://apnews.com/article/oklahoma-teacher-banned-books-2615726cd3e3eb7b04614ea969250f0e?utm_source=copy&utm_medium=share.

Lopez, Brian. 2021. "Republican Bill That Limits How Race, Slavery and History Are Taught in Texas Schools Becomes Law." December 2. *The Texas Tribune*. https://www.texastribune.org/2021/12/02/texas-critical-race-theory-law/.

Markham, Madison, and Samantha LaFrance. 2024. "The State of Book Bans: Utah's 'No-Read'

List." August 22. *PEN America*. https://pen.org/the-state-of-book-bans-utahs-no-read-list/.

Marshall, Tanji Reed, and William Rodick. 2023. "The Search for More Complex Racial and Ethnic Representation in Grade School Books." *EdTrust*. https://edtrust.org/wp-content/uploads/2014/09/Curriculum-Report-FINAL.pdf.

Massie, Victoria M. 2016. "Want to Measure a Film's Diversity? Try the DuVernay Test." February 1. Vox.com. https://www.vox.com/2016/2/1/10888212/duvernay-test-movie-diversity.

PEN America. 2023. "Manuscripts Don't Burn: A Timeline of Literary Censorship, Destruction, and Liberation." July 13. PEN America. https://pen.org/censorship-history-book-bans/.

PEN America. 2023. "Educational Intimidation: How 'Parents' Rights' Legislation Undermines the Freedom to Learn." August 23. PEN America. https://pen.org/report/educational-intimidation/.

PEN America. 2024. "America's Censored Classrooms 2024: Refining the Art of Censorship." October 8. PEN America. https://pen.org/report/americas-censored-classrooms-2024/.

Rinderle, Katherine. 2023. "I Was the First Casualty of Georgia's Anti-Democratic School Book Ban." September 1. *MSNBC Opinion*. https://www.msnbc.com/opinion/msnbc-opinion/georgia-teacher-fired-book-ban-my-shadow-is-purple-rcna102570.

Runnels, Ayden. 2025. "Bill Giving Texas Parents, School Boards More Control Over Library Books Heads to Gov. Greg Abbott." May 26. *Texas Tribune*. https://www.texastribune.org/2025/05/26/texas-school-library-bill/.

Schaeffer, Katherine. 2024. "Key Facts About Public School Teachers in the U.S." September 24. Pew Research Center. https://www.pewresearch.org/short-reads/2024/09/24/key-facts-about-public-school-teachers-in-the-u-s/.

Sipe, Lawrence R., and Anne E. Brightman 2009. "Young Children's Interpretations of Page Breaks in Contemporary Picture Storybooks." *Journal of Literacy Research* 41 (1): 68–103.

Stanovich, Keith E. 2009. "Matthew Effects in Reading: Some Consequences of Individual Differences in the Acquisition of Literacy." *Journal of Education* 189 (1–2): 23–55.

Sun, Yun-Jun, et al. 2024. "Early-Initiated Childhood Reading for Pleasure: Associations with Better Cognitive Performance,

Mental Well-Being and Brain Structure in Young Adolescence." *Psychological Medicine* 54 (2): 359–373.

Tefera, Adai Abebe, Jeanne M. Powers, and Gustavo Fischman. 2018. "Intersectionality in Education: A Conceptual Aspiration and Research Imperative." *Review of Research in Education* 42 (1): vii–xvii.

Tokuda-Hall, Maggie. 2022. *Love in the Library.* Somerville, MA: Candlewick.

Tunnell, Michael O., and James S. Jacobs. 2013. "The Origins and History of American Children's Literature." *The Reading Teacher* 67 (2): 80–86.

Woodson, Jacqueline. 1998. "Who Can Tell My Story?" January 3. *The Horn Book.* https://www.hbook.com/story/who-can-tell-my-story.

INDEX

Page numbers in *italics* denote figures, those in **bold** denote tables.

INDEX

INDEX

CREDITS

Figure 1.1, The Diversity Gap in Children's Books. Produced by LEE & LOW BOOKS. Designed by Ben Mautner. © 2015. Design updated by Elliane Mellet. © 2022. Permission arranged with LEE & LOW BOOKS Inc., New York, NY 10016. All rights reserved. For more conversations on diversity, visit blog.leeandlow.com.

Figures 3.1–3.5, Interior spreads from *IF YOU COME TO EARTH* by Sophie Blackall © 2020 Used with Permission from Chronicle Books LLC, San Francisco.

Figure 4.1, Illustration from *THE SNOWY DAY* by Ezra Jack Keats, copyright © 1962 by Ezra Jack Keats; copyright renewed © 1990 by Martin Pope, Executor. Used by permission of Viking Children's Books, an imprint of Penguin Young Readers Group, a division of Penguin Random House LLC. All rights reserved.

Figure 4.2, Illustration, by Vashti Harrison, copyright © 2019 by Vashti Harrison; and Excerpt(s) from *HAIR LOVE* by Matthew A. Cherry, text copyright © 2019 by Matthew A. Cherry. Used by permission of Kokila, an imprint of Penguin Young Readers, a division of Penguin Random House LLC. All rights reserved.

Figure 4.3, Cover from *JULIÁN IS A MERMAID.* Copyright © 2018 by Jessica Love. Reproduced by permission of the publisher, Candlewick Press, Somerville, MA.

Figure 4.4, Figure 4.5, and Figure 6.1; Cover and illustrations from *When Aidan Became a Brother.* Text copyright © 2019 by Kyle Lukoff. Illustrations copyright © 2019 by Kaylani Juanita. Permission arranged with LEE & LOW BOOKS Inc., New York, NY 10016. All rights reserved. Learn more at leeandlow.com/books/when-aidan-became-a-brother.